POLITICAL
SUICIDE

POLITICAL SUICIDE

MISSTEPS, PECCADILLOES, BAD CALLS, BACKROOM HIJINX,
SORDID PASTS, ROTTEN BREAKS, AND JUST PLAIN DUMB
MISTAKES IN THE ANNALS OF AMERICAN POLITICS

ERIN McHUGH

PEGASUS BOOKS
NEW YORK LONDON

POLITICAL SUICIDE

Pegasus Books LLC
80 Broad Street, 5th Floor
New York, NY 10004

First Pegasus Books edition April 2016

Interior design by Maria Fernandez

Library of Congress Cataloging-in-Publication Data is available.

ISBN: 978-1-60598-978-5

10 9 8 7 6 5 4 3 2 1

Printed in the United States of America
Distributed by W. W. Norton & Company

I want to dedicate this book to the guys in the
white hats—in my life, the Fitzpatrick family:
Senator Jack, Jane, Nancy, and Ann.
You dumped me on a street in Pittsfield in 1973
to ring doorbells and ask for votes, and I began to
understand what service to the people is all about.

CONTENTS

INTRODUCTION

I n the twenty-first century, it seems that the electoral process—
from our local school board elections to campaigns for mayor
and congressman to the selection of the next president of our
fifty states—has become a circus. What should be a serious and
thoughtful activity on which the future of the country rests is
instead filled with budgetary tightrope routines, sparkly partisan
costumes, ethical disappearing acts, and most certainly, clowns.
Instead, it becomes Three Rings of Horror. We are so fatigued
by the time the mud is slung, the skeletons come out of the closet,
and Election Day is over that we're often exhausted by our new
legislators before they've even had a chance to start their jobs.
The bloom is already off the rose, the thrill is gone—and they
haven't even had a chance to screw it up yet.

Oh, but they will. Not all of them, of course, but enough
to keep the headlines full and the 24-hour news programming

churning. Enough will mess up to make us wish we had voted for someone else or to wonder, "How could he think he'd get away with that?" And we'll sit back and shake our heads and say to each other, "Now *that* is political suicide."

Political Suicide is a collection of some of the most incredible stories of misdeeds from our nation's past—an array of tales of human misbehavior as old as time itself. There are all the things we've come to expect from politicians, including bribery, sex scandals, bigotry, embezzlement, and payoffs. But it turns out that there are myriad ways to mess up on the political stage, if one has only a bit of imagination and enough rope to hang one's self: brawls on the chamber floor in Congress; rent boys dressed as Nazis; candidates dressed as Nazis; girlfriends named "Toodles"; stolen money hidden under pillows; candidates who never existed; pistols at dawn; and some who happily sold their souls to the highest bidder. To name but a few.

There are many ways to commit hara-kiri in a government job, and, through the centuries, American politicians have tried them all. Given that it's decidedly difficult today to hide anything from the camera—whether professional paparazzi or ill-advised homemade movies—it's shocking how many politicians try. What's perhaps even more shocking is how much egregious behavior came to light when there was nothing more available than the scratch of a quill by a late-night candle to catalog misdeeds.

If it all weren't so appalling, it would be funny . . . and frankly, sometimes it still is. But it's all part of the story: the fascinating, always evolving (or devolving), ingenious, outrageous story of the American landscape—one crazy politician at a time.

THE MANY FACES OF DEATH

Murder, suicide, and plain old-fashioned duels are not just the stuff of B movies. Throughout America's history, politicians have often found that the only way to solve their problems has been to resort to life-and-death solutions. A lot of it is more than they bargained for when they signed up for a life in the spotlight. From pistols at dawn to high dives and shoot-outs: welcome to the end of the line.

AARON BURR

(1756–1836)

A aron Burr's political ascent was rapid. He moved up from state assemblyman to attorney general and then on to senator from New York State before becoming the third vice president of the United States under once and future superstar Thomas Jefferson. Though Burr was admired by many as a judicious president of the Senate during his term as the country's vice president, Jefferson himself never seemed to be a fan, though he remained mum about his reasons. But the lack of love must have been evident enough to Burr: he ran for governor of New York in 1804, before his first term as vice president was even over. Unfortunately for him, he was handily trounced at the polls.

Any chance at the presidency (or even another term as second-in-command) was scotched when Burr decided to defend his honor by challenging his nemesis—our nation's first secretary of the treasury, Alexander Hamilton—to a duel. Hamilton had been digging at Burr for years; in fact, the vice president insisted Hamilton had been disparaging his honor for more than a decade. But Hamilton made some particularly disparaging comments in the media during Burr's gubernatorial run, and that was the last straw for Burr. After years of needling, Burr decided there was no better solution than pistols at dawn to end their quarrel once and for all. Win or lose, a duel was probably not the best idea. Though fairly commonplace, dueling was still on the books as a crime in both New York and New Jersey—and remains so in many states even today.

The two men faced each other on July 11, 1804, at the Heights of Weehawken in New Jersey. Burr killed Hamilton that morning, of course, but exactly what happened has been long disputed. For many years, historians believed that Hamilton fired first but threw away that shot, a gentlemanly dueling ploy meant to show courage. Historically, it was not unusual for both men to fire and purposefully miss, thus having duly engaged in the duel while letting it end without any bloodshed. However, a 1976 article in *Smithsonian* magazine gave rise to speculation that Hamilton's pistol had been fixed with a hair trigger, giving him a leg up to get off the first shot. This would imply that he may have intended to shoot Burr and simply missed. For his part, Burr seems to have shot to kill. Both men had engaged in duels before and knew the unspoken rules; neither appeared to abide by them that morning. The result was that the vice president was charged with murder in both New York and New Jersey, but eventually the case was dropped.

Aaron Burr didn't meet his maker that day, but his career was certainly buried. Jefferson dumped him from his ticket, and by the next year, Burr was embroiled in even worse trouble: it appeared that while still acting as vice president Burr began to investigate taking over the Louisiana Territory and points west to create his own empire. He was accused of treason, arrested, and indicted for what became known as the Burr Conspiracy; yet he managed once again to escape formal punishment. He died alone in a boardinghouse on Staten Island decades later, which may have been the just end he deserved.

JONATHAN CILLEY

(1802–1838)

P erhaps the pen is mightier—and smarter—than the sword.

Today, one can hardly imagine that insults about a newspaper would lead to anything but a multimillion-dollar lawsuit. In bygone days, however, a duel was the perfect way to get your reputation cleared. Such was the case of Maine congressman Jonathan Cilley and William Graves, his colleague from Kentucky.

Cilley had been born into an old New England family in New Hampshire. He went to college in Maine, at Bowdoin, and then settled down there following graduation. He became a lawyer and hung out his shingle in Thomaston, edited the town paper, and became speaker of the house of the Maine legislature. In 1837, he became a United States congressman. He would be in office less than a year before his death.

When the Twenty-fifth Congress opened in March of 1837, it didn't take Cilley long to stir up trouble. He was displeased with some of the press coverage of the Congressional proceedings, in particular James Watson Webb's work for the *New York Courier and Enquirer.* And so, Cilley spoke up from the House floor, accusing Webb of bribery and calling him corrupt.

Webb was displeased, to say the least. Incensed—and having no way to defend himself in the halls of Congress, as he was not a member—Webb turned to his good friend and fellow Whig, Congressman William J. Graves of Kentucky, and asked Graves to deliver a letter to Cilley. When Cilley refused the letter and went on to make further disparaging remarks about Webb, Graves took this as a direct insult to his own honor, as Webb was his friend. In the spirit of the day, Graves challenged Cilley to a duel.

And so, on February 24, 1838 in Bladensburg, Maryland, the two men faced each other. Cilley had virtually no experience with guns. After the first round, in which both men missed, Cilley told his fellow member of Congress that he bore him no personal ill will; though they were from different political parties, they'd never once had a grievance with each other before. Graves insisted they go a second round. Again, both missed their mark. It was at that point that a gentleman's duel would generally end. But Graves's second egged them on, and the politicians agreed upon a third round. Shots were fired, Cilley was struck in the femoral artery, and he bled to death in less than two minutes.

The three rounds of the duel seemed excessive, and in the aftermath of Congressman Cilley's death—which many Americans considered murder—Congress passed a law against dueling . . . at least in the nation's capital. There was talk of censure for Graves and for both of the seconds at the duel. That never happened, but it does seem that the only person who escaped from the episode without a mark on him was James Watson Webb. Talk about the power of the press.

DANIEL SICKLES

(1819–1914)

D aniel Sickles was a controversial figure from beginning to end, starting with his birth date: though records show it to be 1819, Sickles claimed he was born in 1825, and for good reason—he had a fifteen-year-old fiancée and thought it might help to shave six years off his age, dropping him from thirty-three to twenty-seven. Though Sickles had known Teresa Bagioli nearly all of her life, neither family was keen on the pairing, but they were not to be deterred; the couple was married in 1852. It seemed as if Teresa had picked herself a winner, as Sickles had gone to law school and become a member of the New York State assembly. But she didn't necessarily have a faithful one, as Sickles had a long-standing affair with Jane Funk, a prostitute better known as Fanny White.

Fanny had been a popular New York City prostitute, and the "special friend" of Daniel Sickles's since the 1840s. Long before he made Teresa an honest woman, Sickles had caused many a ruckus with Fanny in tow. When he first entered the Assembly, he took Fanny to Albany with him and even brought her to breakfast at his hotel, shocking many of the other guests. He also brought her to work, and she accompanied him to the Assembly Chamber. (He was censured for that one.) They even had one epic night with Fanny dressed in drag that ended with them both in jail. The two of them were quite a pair. Needless to say, Fanny wasn't pleased when she learned of his marriage to a teenager. But Sickles somehow managed to smooth things over. In fact, when he went to London in the employ of future United States president James Buchanan in 1853, it was Fanny who came along for the wild ride instead of the pregnant Teresa Bagioli Sickles.

But Sickles had one set of rules for himself and apparently another set entirely for his wife. He received an anonymous letter telling him that Philip Barton Key II (son of Francis Scott Key, who wrote the words to "The Star-Spangled Banner") was fooling around with Teresa, and he was furious. When Sickles spotted Key lurking outside his home in Lafayette Park, across from the White House, on February 27, 1859, he ran out, pistol in hand. Reports have it that there was some grappling, and that Key threw his opera glasses at his accuser in defense. But Sickles got the deed done, shooting Key and then yelling, "Is the damned scoundrel dead yet?"

Sickles went to trial, and it's fair to say he got away with murder. Not only that, it was a landmark case: Daniel Sickles was the first person to be acquitted for murder by pleading temporary insanity, claiming he was driven mad by jealousy and anger at his cheating wife. Public opinion was on his side; his wife had been running around, after all. Following the trial, Sickles publicly forgave Teresa and reunited with her. He played hooky from Congress for a bit and stayed out of the public eye, but the love between the couple was not meant to be. They were soon estranged.

As if his scandalous romantic life wasn't enough, controversy of one type or another would follow Sickles for the rest of his life. He entered military service near the start of the Civil War as a political general, a post designed for bigwigs with little or no previous war experience. He recruited a regiment he called the Excelsior Brigade and began to build a brand new reputation. But there were some bumps along the way: Sickles wasn't the best at showing up for his job and, with one excuse after another, happened to miss the Battle of Williamsburg, the Second Battle of Bull Run, and the Battle of Antietam. Nevertheless, President Abraham Lincoln, who had long been a Sickles fan, promoted him to major general, making him the only non–West Point corps commander in the war. But Sickles did not rise to the challenge, and the Battle of Gettysburg would be the end of his career. First, he disobeyed a direct order about his position, putting his men at great risk; then Sickles was hit by a cannonball and subsequently lost a leg. (Always the showman, the bone of his leg is even today on display at the National Museum of Health and Medicine.)

Despite this setback, Sickles was far from finished; he had one more big sex scandal in him. As U.S. minister to Spain from 1869–1873, he had an affair with Queen Isabella, and ended up marrying one of her (very young) ladies in waiting.

He resigned his post and moved to Paris for a few years before finally returning to the United States in 1879. It was then that Daniel Sickles embarked on a new career—which, ironically, turned out to be his most successful.

Though Sickles was given a Medal of Honor in 1897 for boldly commanding his troops at Gettysburg, even with his shattered leg, he would never be able to regain any real military credibility. However, upon his return to New York, he saw that war veterans were returning to the battlegrounds on which they'd fought, in remembrance of their personal experiences. At first, Sickles was only an unofficial raconteur (one can only imagine him making himself the hero of every story), but, in time, the preservation of battlefields became a topic of national import. Sickles, who was once again serving as a congressman, nearly thirty years after his first term, helped to sponsor legislation to form the Gettysburg National Military Park.

Nearly every major general who fought at Gettysburg was honored with a memorial at the battlefield site. Sickles is the rare exception, with nothing there to mark his service in the war, despite his own involvement in the founding of the park itself and all its memorials. Sickles told people he felt that the whole park was a memorial to him. And yet, there actually was a monument commissioned for him—it just never got completed. There is speculation that Sickles scrapped the monument and pocketed the money for himself instead. It wouldn't be outside of the realm of possibility: a few years earlier, he'd been caught embezzling $27,000 from the New York Monuments Commission, But General Daniel Edgar Sickles took that secret to his grave, passing away in 1914 at the age of ninety-four.

PHILEMON T. HERBERT

(1825–1864)

t's one thing to send back food in a restaurant or to leave a paltry tip if dissatisfied with the service. It's another thing entirely to shoot the waiter.

But that was the route Philemon T. Herbert took.

Herbert was born in Pine Apple, Alabama in 1825 into a Southern family, but when he heard about the Gold Rush in the 1840s, he hightailed it out to California. He was elected to Congress there in 1855. It was during a trip to Washington, D.C. the following year that he had his fateful meal.

On the morning of May 8, 1856, Herbert stopped in for breakfast at the Willard, then the best hotel in town. Reports are that Herbert had enjoyed a night out in the nation's capital the evening before. He was a man not averse to a few hands of cards, a trip to a local brothel, and some merry tippling. Thus, when he arrived in the dining room at the Willard on the morning of May 8, 1956, he needed sustenance—and he needed it fast.

The problem was that the Willard dining room served breakfast only until 10:30 A.M., and Herbert arrived past eleven, when the staff had already begun to prepare for the luncheon crowd. By the time Herbert got there, the dining room was nearly empty. There was just one customer, Dutch ambassador Henry Dubois, finishing up his morning meal. A staffer was sent to the kitchen to inquire whether the chef would consider serving Herbert at this late hour. But the congressman—who, according to some reports, appeared still drunk—was impatient and ordered a nearby waiter, Thomas Keating, to get him some breakfast, calling him a "damn Irish son of a bitch." Since someone else had already been dispensed to the kitchen, Keating refused.

Herbert was apoplectic. Crockery was smashed, a chair was thrown, a sugar bowl went flying. It was more like a barroom brawl than a breakfast scene as the two men scuffled in the center of the room. And then Herbert drew a pistol and shot Thomas Keating square in the chest.

Herbert turned himself in that afternoon, was charged with manslaughter, and then set free on bail for $10,000. Later that night, he dined with Philip Barton Key, who, in addition to being the man who fatally courted Daniel Sickles's wife, also happened to be U.S. attorney for the District of Columbia—the very man who would be prosecuting Herbert in court. That's Old Boys' Network at its best (or perhaps worst, depending on how you look at it).

Herbert was indicted for murder, but it never really looked like he was in danger of serving any jail time. A movement to censure and expel him from Congress was tabled. His first trial ended in a hung jury. During his second trial, the judge hinted to the jury members that perhaps Herbert had shot Keating in self-defense. The Dutch ambassador, who had been the lone diner on the scene, pleaded diplomatic immunity and dodged appearing in court at all. The waiters from the dining room—one of whom was Patrick Keating, the murdered man's brother, and all of whom were Irish—were the only ones available to testify, but they faced tremendous class discrimination both in the courtroom and in the newspapers. These were the years just prior to the Civil War, and some of the newspaper coverage of the shooting manifested opinions that the Irish waiters' stature in society was about the same as a free slave. In Alabama, the *Montgomery Advertiser* declared, "There is no doubt he acted in self defense. It is getting time that hotel waiters a little farther north were convinced that they ARE servants, and not gentlemen in disguise. We hope that this affair will teach them prudence." Even the *New York Times* wrote, "Whatever the result, it must be a source of poignant regret to Mr. Herbert and his friends, that he carried arms with him into the hotel breakfast-room, and that even if he found it necessary to assail at all one whose station was so far beneath his own, he should have permitted himself to take the life of his fellow being when a wound in the arm or some other part not vital would have disabled him just as effectually."

Herbert got off scot-free.

Though Philemon Herbert got a free pass east of the Mississippi, when he returned to California, the voters would have none of it. Not only was the citizenry uninterested in seeing him run for Congress again, they didn't even want him living in their state. His constituents eagerly signed a petition asking him to pack up and leave. And so Herbert headed to El Paso, Texas in 1859, where he opened a law office, was elected in 1863 to the Confederate Congress, and then went to war as a lieutenant colonel. He was killed in battle in July of 1864.

ARTHUR BROWN

(1843–1906)

He was a handsome son of a gun, and the ladies must have agreed. He went through enough of them. But Arthur Brown would come to find out that there's nothing more deadly than a lady scorned.

Brown was born in Kalamazoo, Michigan in 1843. After he earned his law degree from the University of Michigan at Ann Arbor, he moved back to his hometown to hang out his shingle. He married a woman, now only known in the annals of time as "Mrs. L. C. Brown," and they had one daughter, named Alice. But soon enough, the lawyer's attentions were diverted by a state senator's daughter, Miss Isabel Cameron. When the affair became public, the Browns separated. The former Missus was not pleased; there are reports that Mrs.

L. C. Brown took a shot at her husband—lucky for him, she missed.

In 1879, Brown moved to Utah. Ten years prior, the Transcontinental Railroad had been finished there at Promontory Summit and new settlers were arriving in droves. Brown had a notion that maybe he had a chance at being U.S. district attorney for the territory. He failed in that quest, but set up a private law practice for himself, and was thrilled when Isabel Cameron packed up and moved to Utah to join him. He got a divorce from Mrs. B. #1 and made Isabel Mrs. B. #2. She soon bore him a son, Max. It was the start of a second chance.

When Utah became the 45th state in the union in 1896, Arthur Brown's political luck changed for the better. Statehood meant there would be United States senators, and Brown was successfully elected one of the first two, and served briefly as a Republican. Through his political work, he met a candidate for Mrs. B. #3: Anna Bradley, secretary of the Republican State Committee and a married mother of two who was thirty years Brown's junior. Anna hung around Brown's office so much that it drove her husband, Clarence, crazy. He left her in 1898, moved to Nevada, was consumed by drinking and gambling, and was eventually arrested for embezzling and jailed. By mid-1899, Anna was pregnant. She gave birth to a baby boy in February of 1900 and named him Arthur Brown Bradley.

Brown, meanwhile, was still married. The present Mrs. Brown, Isabel, had no intentions of giving up her husband. When Brown filed for divorce from Isabel in 1902 and bought Anna Bradley an engagement ring, Isabel retaliated by to hiring a private investigator to follow the pair. Brown and Anna were caught in the act and arrested for adultery; Brown posted bail for them both. Meanwhile, Isabel had gotten her hands on more than three hundred letters from Anna to her husband, and she threatened to release them to the press unless Brown came home. He returned to Isabel and even made an offer to his mistress—money and a house, as a payoff to stay out of their lives—but Anna was steadfast. She replied that she wanted "nothing but the senator." By 1903, Anna had won Brown back, and the dalliance between the two was ablaze full force. At one point, Isabel tracked down the lovers to their hotel room, and managed to grab Anna by the throat and throw her to the floor. Mrs. Brown's lawyer, who happened to be with her, tried to intervene, only to be told, "Let me alone. I will kill her." Following this melee, Brown gave Anna a gun for protection against his wife. Talk about a happy marriage.

In November of 1903, Anna had another son, Martin Montgomery Brown Bradley. Things weren't so great for Anna at this point; she now had four children (the elder two with Clarence), and was raising them alone. She wanted that ring from Brown and threatened to plead guilty in court to the adultery charges (which would mean bringing Brown down with her) unless he admitted paternity of their two children. Brown begged her not to, vowing again to marry her. Anna had had enough of Arthur Brown's empty promises, and went through with her threat, pleading guilty. But Brown, ever the lawyer, knew that Isabel—being his wife—couldn't testify against him, and he managed to get the charges dropped.

And so Brown and Isabel remained married. When Isabel died of cancer in 1905, Brown immediately called Anna and told her it was time for her to get a divorce from Clarence at last, swearing to her, "We will make this matter right." And yet, another year went by. Anna became pregnant again, but lost the child. Brown continued to drag his feet about marriage. When he left Utah to plead a case before the Supreme Court in Washington, D.C., he left Anna a farewell present: a one-way train ticket to California.

No fool she, Anna switched her ticket for one to Washington in order to confront her lover. She took a room at the Raleigh Hotel, where Brown was staying, and, on December 8, 1906, had a maid let her into his room. He wasn't there, but Anna discovered love letters from Annie Adams Kiskadden (mother of famed actress Maude Adams). The letters made it quite clear that Annie believed that *she* was about to be Mrs. B. #3. In fact, they seemed to indicate that Brown and Annie were already engaged.

Anna went back to her room distraught and awaited Brown's return. When she heard him come in that night, she visited his room—equipped with the gun he'd given her to protect herself against Isabel. She fired, and struck him in the abdomen. When the hotel manager arrived on the scene, Brown said simply, "She shot me." He was rushed to the hospital and died several days later, on December 12, 1906.

The case seemed open-and-shut, but the public—and the jury—took pity on Anna. Her cause was helped enormously when it was revealed that four months before his death, Brown had written a new will that had nary a mention of Anna Bradley or her children. He never even admitted to fathering their two sons. Before her trial, Anna said, "That man heaped such indignities upon me that, disgraced, robbed of everything a woman holds dear in this world, and refused amends, there was nothing left for me to do but kill him, to wipe out the stain of shame and disgrace he had placed on my life." And so it was that Anna Bradley was acquitted, and, exhausted and in ill health, moved out west to live with her sister. She held several jobs over the years, never married again, and died at age 77 in 1950.

In a horrifying Cain and Abel–like epilogue to the story, Anna's sons Arthur and Matthew Bradley (one fathered by Clarence, the other by Arthur) argued on a family trip about who would cook and who would do the dishes. Young Arthur stabbed Matthew to death.

HENRY DENHARDT

(1876–1937)

There are some politicians who work a lifetime to cement a legacy for themselves. And there are others, like Henry Denhardt, who are remembered for anything but their political service.

Many say Denhardt deserved more recognition than he got, and they're probably right. He served in both the Spanish-American War and World War I, eventually becoming a brigadier general. He worked as both a prosecutor and a judge and was the 34th lieutenant governor of Kentucky from 1923 to 1927, and went on to become an adjutant general and head of Kentucky's National Guard. He was an honorable man, a hero. Until, that is, it came to late-in-life love.

In 1933, at sixty-one, Denhardt divorced his wife and retired from public life. He moved to an eight-hundred-acre ranch. It was a lonely life, to be sure, but he eventually met and became enchanted with Verna Garr Taylor. Now Taylor was no spring chicken; at forty, she was also divorced, with two nearly grown daughters. But she seemed to be a bit of a catch: she had a successful laundry business of her own and was known, as later reported in *Life* magazine, as "the most beautiful woman in two counties." Some wondered what she saw in the balding, stocky Denhardt. Their courtship nevertheless bloomed, and the couple soon became engaged. Denhardt was a lucky guy—until November 7, 1936, that is.

On the night in question, the couple went for a drive to get a little air. Along the way, Denhardt later said, they had some car trouble and were forced to pull over at the side of the road. Denhardt said that because he didn't feel well, he stayed in the car while Taylor walked to a nearby gas station for help. Two men eventually came back to Denhardt's car and pushed it to the station.

When the gas station owner finally came to examine the car, Taylor was nowhere in sight; Denhardt said she had walked up the road to look for a glove she'd lost. When she didn't return, they went to look for her and found her several hundred feet down the road, dead from a bullet to the heart. The shot had been fired from Denhardt's .45 army revolver, which was kept his glove compartment; the gun was on the ground by her side.

The trial in New Castle, Kentucky, was the highlight of the spring season. More than one thousand spectators turned out, many of them bringing picnics to enjoy on the courthouse lawn. Denhardt vowed from the start that his fiancée had committed suicide; he said she had been upset and depressed because one of her daughters opposed their marriage. But rumor had it that the murder was the fatal result of a love triangle, with the third party being Chester Woolfolk, a handsome 27-year-old Verna had hired as her laundry truck driver. Had Denhardt been jilted and killed Taylor in revenge? The evidence certainly seemed to point that way: though Denhardt said he hadn't fired a gun in six months, powder burns were found on his person. Verna, however, had none, indicating she hadn't handled the weapon. It also emerged at the trial that deep heel marks from Taylor's shoes had been found close to her body at the scene of her death, indicating that she had been involved in a struggle.

Yet despite the evidence, the trial ended in a hung jury. While Denhardt awaited a new trial in the fall, a separate incident came up. Patricia Wilson, a local party girl, had been found dead in an elevator shaft in Louisville the year before; now her family was blaming Henry Denhardt for her death. Though Denhardt claimed to have never met her, it wasn't an ideal allegation to have hanging over his head while he awaited trail on Verna's murder charge.

But fate wasn't satisfied to wait for the jury's verdict. On September 20, 1937, the night before his new trial, Denhardt was leaving his lawyer's office when he was gunned down by the three Garr brothers, Verna's Taylor's siblings, who had laid in wait in order to avenge their sister's murder.

All three men were acquitted of any wrongdoing.

MARION ZIONCHECK

(1901–1936)

Born in Poland in 1901, Marion Zioncheck was but a tot when his family moved to the United States and settled in Seattle, Washington. There he eventually entered politics, first as a left-leaning college student and then as a New Deal Democrat in local politics. By 1932, at the age of thirty-one, he ran for Congress, won, and entered the hallowed halls in Washington, D.C. in 1933.

Early on, Zioncheck showed great promise: he was energetic, interested in reform, an eager and steady worker, and a stalwart advocate for the Great Depression's "forgotten man." He seemed high-spirited, but much of it was chalked up to youthful enthusiasm—after all, he was a bachelor new to the nation's capital, and he had the world to conquer. But the truth was that he was probably bipolar, something that would likely be more quickly diagnosed today but remained untreated in the congressman.

It began with pranks and partying; though excessive, this behavior was hardly unique to Zioncheck. But by 1936, the stories—and the attendant arrests—were multiplying. He made waves for publicly referring to Supreme Court justices as "old fossils." He hosted one legendary New Year's party where the cops were called, only to find when they arrived to investigate the noise complaint that Zioncheck had taken over the building's switchboard and was calling up all of the neighbors. He was also arrested for speeding down Connecticut Avenue at 70 mph; not only did he resist arrest, but he tried to run out of the courtroom upon appearing before the judge and was cited for contempt. And then he found a girlfriend, a Works Progress Administration secretary named Rubye Louise Nix.

She didn't remain a girlfriend for long; they married in a jiffy. Unwilling to wait three days for papers to clear in the District of Columbia, they hopped in the car and drove to Maryland to get hitched. When the groom didn't have the two bucks for the license, he borrowed it from the justice of the peace. Reporters were thrilled, of course: Zioncheck had become their new go-to guy for headlines, and this was a winner. Before departing for his honeymoon, Zioncheck hosted a small coterie of journalists in his apartment. He mixed cocktails while wearing an Indian headdress and entertaining inquiries. When asked how he'd met and married his bride so quickly, he explained, "I met her about a week ago when she called me up one night. She asked me down and so I went down and looked her over. She was OK."

Ain't love grand?

Zioncheck and Rubye then took off to Puerto Rico for a honeymoon, where more wildness ensued. Zioncheck got in two separate car accidents, including one where he bit the driver on the neck and caused their car to crash into a ditch. He also apparently incited a small political riot that got out of hand—so much so that he was forced to call the Marines to intervene. Things were getting out of hand, and it didn't help that he was allegedly tossing back rum-and-hair-tonic cocktails with some abandon.

Upon returning to the mainland, Zioncheck continued his downward spiral. One afternoon, he drove into the White House driveway (yes, you could actually do that then) with some "gifts" for his idol, FDR. The president, fortunately, was not home, so Zioncheck wrote a note and left it behind, along with a bag holding a collection of empty beer bottles, mothballs, and ping-pong balls. Later that day, Zioncheck was arrested and brought to a sanitarium. He escaped several days later, and was picked up again by police. Rubye had him transferred to a different hospital, from which he again escaped—and was arrested and brought back. To gain his freedom, Zioncheck volunteered to return to his hometown of Seattle rather than risk imprisonment in D.C.

Back in Seattle, Zioncheck found he already had quite a fan club. It seemed that people nationwide had loved the crazy stories of the "Capitol Clown"—and none more so than the residents of his home district. They embraced his craziness—it wasn't as if anyone had ever gotten hurt during all of Zioncheck's antics; the guy was just a nut.

When Zioncheck told his constituents he would not run for reelection, a friend, Warren G. Magnuson, filed papers to run for his seat. But suddenly Zioncheck reversed his decision and said he would indeed run again.

Zioncheck, however, would never see the campaign. On their way to a gala on August 7, 1936, Rubye and her husband stopped by his offices in downtown Seattle. While Rubye stayed in the car, Zioncheck went upstairs, wrote a suicide note, and then stepped off the ledge of his window on the fifth floor. His body struck the ground right next to the car in which Rubye sat waiting for him. The hastily scrawled suicide note, written on his official letterhead, read, "My only hope in life was to improve the condition of an unfair economic system that held no promise to those that all the wealth of even a decent chance to survive let alone live."

Was it because his friend had threatened to take his seat? Was it merely the culmination of growing mental instability? We'll never know for sure, but what's clear is that a depressed and very ill Marion Zioncheck felt he had let down the common man and perceived his efforts in politics to be a failure.

Perhaps shockingly, Zioncheck still holds the record for being the only sitting congressman ever sent to an insane asylum.

DOUGLAS R. STRINGFELLOW

(1922–1966)

Americans love to elect former military heroes. So wouldn't status as a retired spy be even better for a political platform?

That tactic seems to have been precisely Douglas R. Stringfellow's modus operandi. In 1952, the then-unknown thirty-year-old World War II veteran ran for Congress as a Republican in Utah, where the seat had been staunchly Democratic for almost two decades. Stringfellow didn't have any previous political experience, but he did have a heck of a story.

On the campaign trail, Stringfellow spoke frequently of his experiences during combat in Europe. He told a horrific tale of being the only surviving soldier of an OSS (Office of Strategic Services) unit. He had parachuted into Germany on a special mission to kidnap a Nazi nuclear scientist, but he was captured, tortured, and held at the German concentration camp at Bergen-Belsen. Incredibly, he escaped, only to be wounded in a mine explosion, an incident that left him laid up in the hospital for months as he battled back from critical injuries. Stringfellow was left a paraplegic and awarded the Silver Star for his bravery.

What a spectacular story! Who wouldn't vote for him? Could it possibly matter that he was a Republican in staunchly Democratic territory? Evidently not, as Stringfellow steamrolled his opponent and won with a whopping 60% of the vote.

The congressman's tale was so impressive that he was asked to be a guest on a popular TV show of the day called *This Is Your Life*. The weekly program's gimmick was to feature a guest who was led to the studio under false pretenses, then surprised with stories and people from their past, making for unexpected reunions, joy, tears—and great ratings. It was a perfect opportunity for Stringfellow, as he was by this time in the throes of his reelection campaign. His prime-time debut was such a hit that he immediately received calls from publishers and Hollywood; now he was truly in the national spotlight.

The problem was that his story wasn't true—and the TV show only brought unwanted attention. The newspaper *Army Times* challenged the ex-soldier's story from top to bottom; there had been no medal, no parachuting, no capture and escape, no spying. Yes, he had been a private in the army and had been injured, but he was not a paraplegic and had always been able to walk with the use of a cane. Quickly, political rivals—mostly eager Democrats—climbed on the finger-pointing bandwagon.

At first, Stringfellow denied all the naysayers. But eventually the burden became too much. He made a public confession, and with only sixteen days left until Election Day, he pulled out of the race. He admitted that he had gotten caught up in his own fame. "I fell into the trap, which in part had been laid by my own glib tongue. I became a prisoner of my own making," Stringfellow said in his confession. "I have made some grievous mistakes for which I am truly sorry."

After his sudden resignation from politics in 1955, Stringfellow tried setting up a speaking tour, but people weren't interested. He did some radio announcing, but under a pseudonym. Finally, he turned to landscape painting. He died at the age of forty-four in 1966.

But that's still not the end of the story. The disgraced politician had written a book, and it sat for decades in a box tied up with a piece of rope. In this autobiography, Stringfellow professed that he grew to actually believe the stories he was telling. His widow and children now insist his lies stemmed from post-traumatic stress disorder. In 2013, the family started a Kickstarter campaign to publish the autobiography. The mocked-up future volume pictured on its Kickstarter page was titled "STRINGFELLOW: The Untold Story of History's Most Controversial War Hero and Politician." The campaign raised a paltry $551 and did not meet its goal. Douglas Stringfellow's book remains unpublished.

R. BUDD DWYER

(1939–1987)

I magine that your entire life—your legacy, all any-body remembers about you—is winnowed down to the moment you died. That was the terrible fate of R. Budd Dwyer.

R. Budd Dwyer led the kind of life that seemed the embodiment of Americana: college, followed by a wife and two kids—a boy and a girl—and a job as a high school social studies teacher and football coach. When he decided to go into politics, his campaigns were run on the promise of integrity. Dwyer was promptly elected and spent five years as a Republican state representative starting in 1965, before jumping over to the state senate for a decade. He was then elected state treasurer of Pennsylvania in 1981.

It was in 1983 that Dwyer's troubles started. There had been a financial misstep predating his administration: The Commonwealth of Pennsylvania had been paying too much on state-related FICA taxes, and rebates amounting to as much as $40 million would need to be paid out to citizens statewide. Dwyer was authorized by the governor to find an accounting firm to right the wrong and distribute the money. The contract was given to a California-based company called Computer Technology Associates (CTA), run by a former Pennsylvanian named John Torquato Jr. But, before long, the governor of the Keystone State received an anonymous tip that CTA had gotten the contract because of a bribe.

Suddenly all eyes were on Budd Dwyer, who, it was alleged, agreed to a bribe of $300,000 to assure that CTA got the bid. As the United States attorney began to investigate, others were brought up on charges as well, including CTA owner Torquato, Torquato's lawyer, William T. Smith, and Smith's wife and law partner, Judy. Republican State Committee chair Bob Asher was also charged. The allegation was that Torquato and the Smiths arranged to offer bribes to Asher and Dwyer to secure the FICA job.

As the investigation heated up, the prosecutor approached William Smith and promised he wouldn't prosecute his wife Judy at all—and might offer William a plea deal, too—if he cooperated with the prosecutors. Meanwhile, Torquato was making the same deal to testify against Smith. It was a finger-pointing jamboree, and Budd Dwyer was at the center of it.

Though Smith insisted that he had offered the bribe to Dwyer and that Dwyer had agreed to it, the prosecutor was forced to admit that no money ever changed hands, which made the case much weaker. Still, on December 18, 1986, Dwyer was convicted of eleven counts of conspiracy, mail fraud, perjury, and interstate transportation in aid of racketeering. He would await sentencing in January of 1987.

Budd Dwyer proclaimed his innocence throughout his ordeal, even, at one point, writing a heartrending letter to President Reagan requesting a presidential pardon. In his letter, he claimed he had not been judged by a jury of his peers, and he argued that Smith had flip-flopped on his testimony about whether or not he had offered Dwyer the bribe. As with all his other pleas to many less powerful people, he received no help.

So on January 22, 1987, the day before his sentencing, Budd Dwyer called a press conference in his office. (Due to a loophole in the law, Dwyer was allowed to keep his job until his sentencing.) Reporters arrived expecting a farewell speech. Dwyer read a speech he had prepared, once again professing his innocence and citing his fears:

> Judge Muir is also noted for his medieval sentences. I face a maximum sentence of 55 years in prison and a $300,000 fine for being innocent. Judge Muir has already told the press that he, quote, "felt invigorated" when we were found guilty, and that he plans to imprison me as a deterrent to other public officials. But it wouldn't be a deterrent because every public official who knows me knows that I am innocent; it wouldn't be a legitimate punishment because I've done nothing wrong."

After his speech, Dwyer took out three envelopes and handed them to three members of his staff: one was a letter to his wife; the second contained his organ donor card and other legal documents; and the third held a letter to the new governor of Pennsylvania. Dwyer then opened a manila envelope and took out a .357 Magnum. As shocked visitors started to protest and approach him, Dwyer put his hand out and said, "This will hurt someone." He put the barrel in his mouth and fired. He died instantly.

TV reporters at the scene had captured Budd Dwyer's suicide on tape, and some stations broadcast the entire sequence. Dwyer's suicide has been immortalized on the Internet, replayed by the media, studied in universities, and obsessed over in documentaries. It's even the subject of a song by the rock band Filter, even though the song, titled "Hey Man, Nice Shot," is frequently incorrectly associated with Kurt Cobain.

As for the sentencing Dwyer had so dreaded, William Smith ultimately received only a year and a day for the identical charges Dwyer had faced; he had feared fifty-five years and a fine of $300,000.

In 2010, filmmaker James Dirschberger took on the story of Budd Dwyer in his documentary *Honest Man: The Life of R. Budd Dwyer*. In the film, William Smith—who, it should be noted, has changed his story several times over the years—said that he gave false testimony under oath against Dwyer as a part of his plea bargain with the prosecutor. "He's dead because of me," Smith said in the film. "To the day I die, I'll regret that I did it."

DAN WHITE
(1946–1985)

"Perhaps the most hated man in San Francisco history."

That's how *San Francisco Weekly* described former city supervisor Dan White more than thirty years after his death, a legacy earned following his assassination of Harvey Milk.

On paper, Dan White looked like a stand-up guy: high school valedictorian, Vietnam War paratrooper, a former police officer and firefighter. He was a conservative man, both in his politics and his morals; he liked things to be black and white. There were reports that White had quit the police department after he saw a fellow officer attack a suspect. It was also said that he left his elected job as a city supervisor partly because of ethical questions he had on the job.

In 1977, Democrat Dan White was voted onto the San Francisco Board of Supervisors on his first try. He was sworn in on the same day—January 8, 1978—as Harvey Milk, well-known throughout the City by the Bay as an activist in the burgeoning gay and lesbian movement. The two new board members could not have been more different: White was the social conservative backed by his former brothers in the police and fire departments, and white, middle-class family types; Harvey Milk was outspoken and sometimes outrageous, already famous nationwide for being the first openly gay man to be voted into public office. Their vast differences resulted in a somewhat tumultuous working relationship.

Reporters, meanwhile, loved the two sparring supervisors. Though in fact they often agreed on city issues, when they did not, it was great press. Before they even took office, they were often paired on local talk shows together, speaking about their differences and their hopes for working in tandem for San Francisco's future. But hopes were one thing and reality was something else. White supported Dianne Feinstein's election as President of the Board, while Milk did not. The two also locked horns on the question of a juvenile offenders facility proposed for White's district, which he was fighting. Still, they weren't always on opposing sides. White supported Milk's gay rights ordinance for the city, an early and important fight that received national attention. And when White's new baby was christened, Harvey Milk was one of only three people from City Hall to be invited.

By the summer of 1978, however, Dan White had begun to change. He was often depressed, and his usual regimen fell by the wayside: he had stopped exercising, was having trouble sleeping, and he'd begun to forgo the healthy eating habits he'd always followed in favor of junk food. It seemed like perhaps politics simply didn't agree with White. He did not enjoy the sport of high-stakes wheeling and dealing, and worse, said he simply couldn't provide for his family on the $9,600 annual salary he received as supervisor. (Money was tight; his only other means of support was a failing baked potato stand down on the wharf.) On November 10, he went to Mayor George Moscone and resigned. A bonus of White's leave-taking was that Moscone could pick a more liberal replacement for his seat, tipping the scales in that direction 6–5. This was a political win for both the Mayor and Supervisor Milk.

Just over a week later, Dan White changed his mind about not being a city supervisor; he wanted his old job back. He went to Moscone and pleaded his case, and the Mayor promised that he'd consider it. But ultimately, with pressure from liberal city supervisors—including Milk—Moscone denied White his seat.

This was not what White wanted to hear. And so on November 27, a distraught and armed Dan White entered City Hall through a window, so as to avoid the metal detectors. He went to Mayor Moscone's office and begged for another chance. When Moscone refused, White killed his former boss with four gunshots. He then walked over to Harvey Milk's office and shot him five times. After shooting, White simply walked out of City Hall and then went to his old precinct and confessed.

White was charged with first-degree murder with special circumstance; this charge came with the possibility of the death sentence. With his confession, the case seemed open-and-shut—a slam-dunk guilty verdict for sure. But White's defense team had a trick up their sleeve that stunned everyone in the court: they claimed the former politician was so depressed at the time of the shootings that he had been acting in a state of diminished capacity. If this were true, then premeditation—a necessary condition for a first-degree murder charge—was off the table. White's lawyers insisted that his depression was evidenced, in part, by his new bad eating habits, including lots of junk food. Only once did they use the snack cake Twinkies as an example, but the press took the "Twinkie Defense" and ran with it. The moniker was to become the watchwords of the trial.

Such a defense seemed so unlikely as to be laughable, but, shockingly, the jury agreed with White's defense team and the diminished capacity argument. Dan White was charged with voluntary manslaughter and sentenced to seven years. Many believed White had gotten away with murder. Much of the gay community took the lenient punishment as a personal attack and, in fact, the case was integral to California's decision to rid itself of the diminished capacity law, which it did in 1982.

Dan White was paroled in January of 1984 after serving just five years of his sentence, and moved to Los Angeles for a year, on parole and under the radar. His plan was to move back to San Francisco, where he still had family, when his parole was over. When Mayor Dianne Feinstein (who had inherited the office upon George Moscone's murder) heard of his intention to come back, she publicly begged him not to return to the city.

White did come back, but he was now perhaps an even more broken man than before. The family he'd returned to had fallen apart, and his marriage was soon over. On October 21, 1985, he went into his garage, got into his car, and committed suicide by carbon monoxide poisoning.

Upon Dan White's death, San Francisco police chief Cornelius Murphy gave a statement to the *New York Times*: "I hope it's the last chapter. I don't think that this is the kind of book that's been written that needs an epilogue. It's time to close the book on Dan White. Let the White family and the City and County of San Francisco get on with its business."

Harvey Milk had once said, "If a bullet should enter my brain, let that bullet destroy every closet door." His death did indeed do much to draw attention to the cause of gay rights. And so, quite unwittingly, Dan White helped change the course of gay history.

MONEY & FINANCES

★ ★ ★

Filthy lucre—sometimes it seems that's all politics is about. That money makes the world go 'round is no news to most people, but the lengths to which it dominates the political sphere is sometimes hard to comprehend. But political success is not necessarily tied to good financial management skills. Whether they hid it, stole it right from under their constituents' noses, or simply had too much of it to begin with, more than one politician has been taken down by the almighty dollar.

CALEB LYON

(1822–1875)

A Staten Island boy, Caleb Lyon certainly seemed early on in life to be a promising national political star. He graduated from college in 1841, and by 1847 he had been appointed the U.S. consul to Shanghai. It was a pretty fast track for someone so young. But soon after his arrival in China, Caleb Lyon decided a life in the Far East wasn't for him. He kept the title, but passed on his duties to a deputy and came back to the United States via South America.

California seemed to be the next big thing happening, and so Lyon headed there, eager to get involved with organizing the bid for statehood. He joined the California constitutional convention, and made such an impact there that he has long been credited with designing the state seal, though the truth is it was created by Robert S. Garnett (who would go on to make his own mark on history by being the first general officer killed in the Civil War).

But California didn't satisfy him either, and in 1849 Lyon returned to New York. By the near year, he was elected to the State Assembly and became a big supporter of the plan to build the Erie Canal, but he resigned when faced with opposition to the project. Ever resilient, he was almost immediately elected to the State Senate, then, in 1853, he parlayed that into a seat in Congress. But New York would not be Caleb Lyon's last political stop, and he served but one congressional term before President Lincoln personally appointed him the governor of Idaho Territory in 1864. In the next step of what was already a dizzying political career, Lyon headed back west.

Lyon didn't hold the governorship for long, but he did manage to make a fine mess of it in the short time he was in office. He seemed to be spectacularly poorly suited for the position; Lyon was an East Coast intellectual—he fancied himself a poet and art critic—not a rough-and-tumble cowboy type. His new constituency didn't really take to him, and Lyon surely didn't do himself any favors when he decided to move the state capital from Lewiston to Boise, declaring that a large city would be a better spot. And then there were the diamonds—or, more exactly, the lack of diamonds. Governor Lyon set off a mini-gem rush when he announced that Idaho was diamond country. He claimed a prospector had found several sizeable stones that were just a taste of what Idaho had to offer. The reality, however, was that just a single large stone had been discovered. Lyon took to carrying a piece of quartz and showing it around, claiming it was a local diamond. Prospectors flocked to what would come to be called "Diamond Gulch," but they found very little.

A crucial part of Lyon's job as governor was to oversee the Indian tribes in the territory. Most importantly, he was tasked with negotiating reservation lands and treaties between the different tribes and the United States government. But here, too, Lyon proved to be something of a snake oil salesman. Promises were made and never kept; treaties were drawn up and never signed. Then one day, Lyon packed up for what he said was a duck hunting trip with some friends, got in a canoe on the Snake River—and skipped town.

It was back East for Caleb Lyon again, and Clinton DeWitt Smith, who had been territorial secretary under Lyon, took over as acting governor in Idaho. Within months, however, Smith was dead, having keeled over during a game of chess. Following an eleven-month absence, Lyon was reappointed governor of the Idaho Territory and was back out West. He made better headway with the Indians and their relationship with the white settlers this time around, but even when his term was over, Lyon's troubles were not. There was a matter of some missing money—more than $41,000 intended for the federal superintendent of Indian Affairs in Washington, D.C. Lyon swore up and down it had been stolen from under his pillow while he was asleep on a train en route to Washington to give the money to the federal superintendent of Indian Affairs. The money never turned up, but as luck would have it, it was bonded, so the government eventually got it back, and "whoever" stole it had a nice little payday. And without proof of any actual wrongdoing, Caleb Lyon went scot-free once more. He returned at last to Staten Island, perhaps with a little extra cash for his high-living, cultured ways, and passed away, unprosecuted, in 1875.

JAMES WILLIAM TATE

(1831–?)

H onest Dick" they called him—a nod to his sterling
reputation. He must have been laughing all the way
to the bank.

James William Tate was Kentucky born and bred, schooled
in the Blue Grass State until he was seventeen. His first job
right out of high school was as a clerk in the local post office;
he must have had a way with the mail, because in 1854—just
ten years later—Tate was named assistant secretary of state
in Kentucky. He stayed in the job for a year, until the next
political administration came in, and then was reappointed to
the position again in 1859. After a two-year turn as assistant
clerk in the Kentucky House of Representatives, Tate was
elected state treasurer in 1867, thus beginning a sweet ride

of easy reelection every other year for two decades. "Honest Dick" was on a roll.

Tate was affable, a hail-fellow-well-met kind of guy, and no wonder: as time and circumstance proved, he was easy with a loan—and often easier on the payback (as in, never). So everything was a breeze for Tate until a gubernatorial candidate suggested that the state accounts should be scrutinized, "Honest Dick" or not. Good idea, thought the state government, which asked Tate to ready his books for inspection. Tate agreed, but cautioned that it would take him some time to get things in order. He successfully delayed for over a year, but of course he knew his fate was inevitable.

Because "Honest Dick," in fact, was not. Behind the genial facade was a gambling man who had made several land and mine investments, many of them unsuccessful— and had no qualms about using deceit to cover it up. But his lies were so good—and his reputation so unsullied—that even when a clerk in the Treasury office saw Tate loading up two large bags with gold, silver, and a giant roll of paper money, he assumed it was all company business, and didn't mention it to anybody. This was Honest Dick, after all! Later on, some employees said they did notice that cash deposits over the last weeks had slowed down to almost nothing, and that almost all incoming monies were in the form of checks, which was very unusual—but it was Honest Dick! His Treasury Department colleagues still were not suspicious when they found a note on Tate's desk saying he had gone to Louisville and would be back in two days. What would become known in the press as "The Great Absconding" had been set into motion.

It became clear after several days that Tate was gone—possibly for good. His wife and daughter had not heard from him since he left, and so officials took matters into their own hands at last and began to investigate. The ledgers were a mess: not only were most of them indecipherable, but the sheer volume of IOUs, old loans, salary advances, "cold checks" from accounts with insufficient funds, and embarrassing loans to former state elected officials was staggering. It looked as if more than $247,000 was gone (about $6 million today), but the books were in such disarray it may well have been more.

The elected officials of Kentucky realized they had been fooled. Less than a week after he disappeared, the governor suspended Dick Tate from his job, but the Treasurer was long gone, of course. He had been spotted drinking heavily in Cincinnati a few days after his disappearance, but that was the last confirmed sighting. A $5,000 reward was offered for his capture, but to no avail. He was convicted in absentia, and the Kentucky state constitution passed a law to impose a one-term limit on all elected officials, in order to keep a closer watch on malfeasance. The law remained intact until 1992, when it was finally bumped up to two terms.

For a long time, the "Honest Dick" Tate trail went cold. But after several years had passed, his daughter Edmonia admitted that she had received a flurry of letters from her father for a short time, starting as soon as a month after his disappearance. The letters were posted from British Columbia, Japan, China, and San Francisco. One letter to Edmonia expressed interest in a pardon so that he could return to Kentucky and name his coconspirators. A group of Kentuckians started a petition to present to the governor for him to do so, but interest was lackluster and the proposal quietly died. There were reports of Honest Dick sightings in China and Brazil in later years, and even at the Chicago World's Fair in 1893. But Edmonia turned out to be the only one who saw any money: in 1898 she managed to finally have her father declared legally dead and collected his insurance policy.

GERALDINE FERRARO

(1935–2011)

B efore there was Sarah Palin, there was Geraldine Ferraro—America's first female candidate for vice president from a major party.

A three-term congresswoman from New York, Ferraro was chosen as former vice president Walter Mondale's running mate in 1984. She had a strong track record in the House as a staunch defender of legislation protecting equal pay for women, and in addition to being the first serious woman candidate for VP, she was also the first Italian-American to get a nomination. "The daughter of an immigrant from Italy has been chosen to run for vice president in the new land my father came to love," Ferraro said from the podium of the Democratic Convention in San Francisco in her history-making acceptance speech. Initial polling was strong, and it certainly seemed like the Mondale-Ferraro ticket could make it all the way to the White House.

The honeymoon wasn't to last. Ferraro faced criticism of her relative lack of foreign policy experience. The Catholic Church was outraged that she—an avowed Roman Catholic herself—held pro-choice views. The *New York Post* got busy digging up dirt on her father's past as a numbers runner. But the worst was yet to come.

As happened later with Palin, whose fitness for the VP spot came into question, Ferraro had been breezily vetted in a process that included a cursory 48-hour glance into her family finances. Ferraro's husband, John Zaccaro, was something of a real estate magnate, and it wasn't long before news surfaced about some questionable loans and contributions from his businesses to her campaign. Ferraro insisted that their financial lives were separate, even though she practiced law from Zaccaro's offices and was listed as an officer of his corporation—which had suspiciously low holdings of under $15,000. There were demands to see their tax filings, and the Republicans went at her particularly hard, knowing that they could get away with criticizing her finances without seeming like they were going after her for her gender.

Whether it was the finances, the media, the Catholic Church, or just plain old indifference to the candidates, none of it helped the Mondale-Ferraro ticket, and they lost by a landslide to the Reagan-Bush team. It certainly didn't help matters when a New York–based politician shrugged off financial irregularities by saying, as Ferraro did, "You people married to Italian men, you know what it's like."

RITA CRUNDWELL

(1953–)

I t's the biggest embezzlement scam you've never heard of. In fact, Rita Crundwell's case is the biggest municipal fraud in American history. And it took place in a little dot on the map known as Dixon, Illinois.

Before Crundwell brought it into the spotlight, Dixon was most famous for being Ronald Reagan's childhood home. The town had just three full-time city employees, and Rita Crundwell, as comptroller and treasurer, was one of them. The majority of employees were part-time and held other jobs to keep their financial heads above water. The mayor made only $9,600 a year, the commissioners, just $2,700.

Crundwell started as a secretary to the mayor right out of high school in 1974 and was appointed to her city financial post in 1983. It was a sweet deal for her. Crundwell was a horse lover and eventually became was one of the best Quarter Horse breeders in the country. Her equine business took up several months a year on the road, going off to horse shows and the like; it was certainly more than her paid four weeks of vacation allowed. But the small-town comptroller had a luxury motor home she traveled around in, and was generally on call for her town duties, even if she was away. The folks of Dixon figured they had a pretty good deal, as Crundwell docked her own pay when she took time off and still was available for work by phone or email.

No one was quite sure how Crundwell afforded the fancy motor home and swanky horse farm in addition to some pricey clothes, furs, and jewelry on her $83,000 annual salary (minus deductions for the pay she docked herself for time off), but everyone knew she sold lots of horses. They figured that's where all her money and her three homes came from. Others assumed she had inherited money from somewhere, despite the fact that the townspeople knew her parents, who were local people and not at all wealthy. People see what they want to see and they believed that Rita Crundwell was trustworthy. She was one of them. And so they didn't question it.

Therefore it came as quite a shock when, in 2011, Kathe Swanson, Crundwell's assistant, discovered a strange bank account when she was covering at the office during one of Crundwell's many absences—an account that had been opened back in 1990. It was named RSCDA, for Reserve Sewer Capital Development Account, and Rita Crundwell was the sole signatory on the account, with the City of Dixon as the primary account holder. The secondary account holder? "RSCDA c/o Rita Crundwell."

The scam was fairly simple: Crundwell would draw up fake invoices, then transfer money from the legitimate City of Dixon bank account—the Capital Development Account—and deposit the money into the dummy account. Any audit would have unearthed the scam, but no one ever checked. Why would they? Rita had worked for the town—for them—all these years! And so Crundwell got away with writing nearly two hundred of these fake "invoices" for road repairs and other items, in addition to checks from the city account to the RSCDA account that were made out directly to "Treasurer." Even some checks made out to equestrian facilities and spas had escaped detection; since no one was watching, no one was noticing.

It started small, but just a few years after opening the account, Rita Crundwell was making checks out fairly regularly for amounts like $300,000, even $500,000. Over the course of thirty years, Rita Crundwell stole $53 million from the town of Dixon, which meant money right out of the pockets of her friends and neighbors. At the same time Crundwell was filling her coffers, the city of Dixon often couldn't afford even the most basic fixes and updates. The police cars all used old radios. There were streets that badly needed repair. There was a water treatment facility that didn't get built.

When Swanson found the dummy account, she was floored. She immediately brought it to the attention of Mayor James G. Burke, who wasted no time in calling in the FBI. Six months later they were ready, and one morning in April 2012 Rita Crundwell was called into Mayor Burke's office, where the FBI was waiting for her.

Crundwell confessed—after she was caught red-handed, that is—and fully cooperated with the FBI. During sentencing, her lawyer asked for leniency, saying she would have to endure "shame and disrepute" for the rest of her life. But the former trusted small-town employee was sent away for twenty years. Dixon, Illinois had paid for three decades of Crundwell's luxurious lifestyle, and now she'd have to pay the price. She is due for release in 2030.

SLAVERY, BIGOTRY & RACISM

★ ★ ★

Since the early days of our country, we have fought, not just for our independence, but too often among our own citizenry for the equality and dignity we each deserve. The first American century was scarred by slavery, but even when the laws changed, too often the hatred stayed with us. Whether it's race, religion, equality of the sexes, or any other kind of discrimination, it's one battle that is far from over.

RICHARD M. JOHNSON

(1780–1850)

I t's hard to hate a hero. And Vice President Richard M.
Johnson was surely that. He had a stellar career in the War
of 1812, topped off by the fact that it was widely rumored
he had been the man who personally killed Chief Tecumseh
of the Shawnee. His political future looked bright: before the
war, he had been a member of Congress, and following his
service, he went back to Kentucky to retake his congressional
seat and reunite with his family, a wife named Julia and their
two daughters. Although the fact was that Johnson had never
married Julia Chinn—she was his common law wife. It would
be illegal to marry her, as Julia was his slave.

Chinn was an octoroon—one-eighth African, seven-
eighths European—and she lived with Johnson and bore

him two daughters, Adeline and Imogene. In the South, a relationship between a white man and a black woman was not so unusual, although the man was most often married to a white woman and openly kept a black mistress, as in Thomas Jefferson's case. But to Johnson's credit, his relationship with Julia was completely above board; she acted as his partner and hostess. When Johnson was away, Julia ran his businesses and farm; she was even by his side at a barbecue at their home for five thousand guests while entertaining the Marquis de Lafayette.

Johnson was eager for a more prestigious job in Washington, and in 1819, he was elected U.S. senator from Kentucky. He continued to bring his wife and daughters out publicly in Southern society, but now, in a position with more visibility, he began to experience some backlash about his relationship with Julia. That backlash was likely the reason he lost his bid for reelection in 1828.

In 1833, Julia Chinn died of cholera. Three years later, with Johnson back in Congress, Martin Van Buren took him on as his vice presidential running mate in 1836. Johnson had the Tecumseh card going for him, which was a plus, but criticism of his relationship with the now-deceased Julia Chinn still followed him. When the Electoral College cast its votes, Van Buren was elected, but Johnson fell one short of a majority. It was the one time in history that the Senate had to invoke the Twelfth Amendment in order to vote Johnson in as vice president.

Richard Johnson's single term as vice president never made headlines. President Van Buren didn't have much use for him; it's said he likely never confided in him, nor asked for his counsel at all. The Democrats permanently turned their backs on him, in part because of the whiff of scandal that still floated behind him from his relationship with Julia. Following the Panic of 1837, the vice president took a leave of absence and went back to Kentucky, essentially to the career for which he had worked so hard. He opened a tavern and spa to help pay his bills, and from all reports, rather liked his new life. After a failed attempt to get his senate seat back and a feeble run for president, Johnson returned to the Kentucky House of Representatives in 1850. But he was ill, a ghastly shadow of his former self; he suffered a stroke and died just weeks later, on November 19, 1850.

Johnson was certainly brave to live a life so openly with Julia and his daughters (who both went on to marry white men) in a country where miscegenation was a law on the books until 1967. But when his wife died, she still died a slave; he had never freed her. After Julia's death, he took up with a member of her family. And when he discovered she had stepped out on him, he sold her.

JAMES HENRY HAMMOND

(1807–1864)

When a person is a politician with a scandalous sex life, it's a bad idea to write it all down. But that's exactly what James Henry Hammond—one-time congressman, senator, and governor of South Carolina—did.

In 1831, Hammond married seventeen-year-old Catherine Elizabeth Fitzsimmons, a girl who was short on good looks but long on money, which suited him just fine. The union gained him access to the plantation set, several stately homes, and more than three hundred slaves.

It's clear—from Hammond's own documentation—that he went outside the marriage for sexual satisfaction. Hammond's letters and diaries plainly showed that he liked the ladies. And teenagers. And men. There were sexually explicit letters of a homosexual nature from 1826 to a college friend named Thomas Jefferson Withers. There were diary entries detailing his sexual abuse of his four of his nieces—all of whom had their reputations so badly sullied that not one of them was ever able to marry. He also recorded affairs he had with slaves he owned, including two who were mother and daughter. His extremely long-suffering wife eventually gave him an ultimatum that he end those relationships, and when he refused, she left him for several years, though they were later reunited.

Evidence of all of this came to light in 1981, when writer and gay historian Martin Duberman found the letters to Withers in a collection of Hammond family papers held by the library at the University of South Carolina. Duberman published them in an essay about homosexual relationships in the pre–Civil War South. Then in 1989, history scholar Carol K. Bleser edited and published *Secret and Sacred: The Diaries of James Henry Hammond, a Southern Slaveholder.* The volume is shocking in so many ways—not just because of the revelation of the full extent of Hammond's sexual proclivities, but because of his behavior as a slave owner as well. Though Hammond believed himself to be benevolent and said one of his greatest "consolations" was that "my negroes . . . love and appreciate me," he was a horrific master and his slaves suffered a higher than usual mortality rate.

Hammond was a stout defender of slavery, a sentiment best demonstrated in his famous "Cotton is King" speech to the U.S. Senate in 1858, in which he defended the practice by saying: "In all social systems there must be a class to do the menial duties, to perform the drudgery of life. . . . It constitutes the very mudsill of society." He went on to utter the climax of the speech with these oft-repeated words: "You dare not make war on cotton—no power on earth dares make war upon it. Cotton is king."

Hammond resigned as the United States senator from South Carolina when the South seceded from the Union. Of course, the Civil War would also have ended his career as a slave owner as well—but Hammond died in 1864, one year before the war was over.

JAMES THOMAS HEFLIN

(1869–1951)

Whatever can be said about James "Cotton Tom" Heflin, it's certainly true that he was a man who loved his mother. For Heflin is perhaps most commonly known as the "Father of Mother's Day."

Actually, Heflin didn't invent the day himself, but he was happy to take credit for it, as he had introduced the resolution in the House. It was the brainchild of a Philadelphia woman named Anna Jarvis, who wrote to politicians and newspapermen after her own mother died in 1905, suggesting a national holiday would be in order. After Congress rejected the original proposal in 1908, Heflin successfully reintroduced the resolution in 1914, and President Woodrow Wilson proclaimed the second Sunday in May to be set aside for the glorification and adoration of mothers. Heflin sported the achievement as a lifelong feather in his cap, which was ironic, as he consistently opposed women's suffrage. It was okay to love your mother, he seemed to think—you just didn't want her to have the right to vote.

In fact, Heflin's overall record on equality was a poor one. After stints as mayor of Lafayette and an Alabama state representative, he was appointed secretary of state of Alabama in 1902. In that role, he helped draft a state constitution that outlawed black Alabamans from voting. He also promoted convict leasing, a post–Civil War anomaly that was dying out elsewhere in the country, but lasted in Alabama until 1928. This practice took convicts (and sometimes black men who had been wrongfully arrested and convicted) and sold them to private parties to use as workers. Technically, it was modern-day slavery, but Heflin defended it, claiming, "God Almighty intended the negro to be the servant of the white man."

In 1904, Heflin entered Congress. Four years into his sixteen-year stint, he decided it was time to segregate the streetcars in the District of Columbia, as was the practice in Alabama. Many of his fellow politicians were horrified at the idea, and his proposal was rejected, so he may have had some residual ill feelings when, one day not long afterward, the Congressman got into an altercation with a black man riding on his streetcar. Though reports of the incident vary widely, Heflin claimed the black man was drinking liquor, swearing, and causing a general disturbance for fellow passengers. Heflin in particular objected to a nearby female passenger being sub-jected to the man's uncouth behavior, so he took out a gun and tried to shoot the black passenger; he missed and shot a tourist instead. There were no legal repercussions, but it was another mark on his already dicey reputation.

Of course, "Cotton Tom" did have his fans. He was a staunch defender of the Alabama cotton farmers, hence the nickname. He had a way with words, speaking passionately and eloquently in support of the crop: "Cotton is a child of the sun; it is kissed by the silvery beams of a southern moon, and bathed in the crystal dew drops that fall in the silent watches of the night." Heflin moved a lot of people with his over-the-top verbiage. As one of his supporters said, "He can take any two words you mention and turn them into the Declaration of Independence, and have enough left over to write the Book of Revelations." Heflin was larger than life on the House floor—and a sight to behold. Among the dour, dark-coated politicians all around him, Heflin looked like he was preparing for a day at the races: white linen suits and big bowties in summer, gorgeous double-breasted waistcoats, striped trousers, and spats in the colder weather. Dapper.

That he was a member of the Ku Klux Klan didn't make much of a difference to the majority of Heflin's white constituency, and Heflin's political career flourished as he set his sights on a spot on the national political stage. In 1920, he got it, via a vacancy created by the death of Senator John H. Bankhead. Heflin was elected to fill the seat, and was then reelected for a full term in 1924.

But instead of building a national profile for himself, Heflin managed to get wrapped up in a newfound hate for the Catholic Church. First, he alleged there was a Catholic working at the Bureau of Printing and Engraving who was behind the design of the new one-dollar bill; Heflin was absolutely sure there were rosary beads drawn around Washington's head. (Nope. Filigree.) Then, he complained in Congress that the new White House drapes were Cardinal red—a sure sign that the arm of the Vatican was so long that it influenced presidential decorating decisions. With the help of the Ku Klux Klan, Heflin started hosting anti-Catholic meetings across the country. He was so incensed by the 1928 presidential run of the Catholic governor of New York, Alfred E. Smith, that he headed up to New York State and railed vehemently against Smith and the local Democrats who supported him. Heflin got what he wanted, as Smith lost to Herbert Hoover, but in the meantime, Heflin had lost the support of his Democratic brethren in Washington.

When reelection time came for Tom Heflin in 1930, he did not retain his seat. He had crossed the line by backing Hoover, and the Democrats in Alabama finally shut him down, refusing to support him. Heflin blamed corruption and fraud, but his complaints were dismissed. He ran for office several times over the next years, but "Cotton Tom" was washed up. He held a few government jobs thrown his way—special assistant this or that—and died back in Lafayette in 1951. *Life* magazine said upon his demise, "You might say that his only lasting service was in being around long enough to be outgrown."

THEODORE G. BILBO

(1877–1947)

Trouble always seemed to be just around the corner for Theodore Bilbo. He was a small man, just five foot two, and whether it was because of his Napoleon complex or a powerful propensity for hate, Bilbo often had his dukes up throughout his long political career from 1908 until his death in 1947—as state senator, lieutenant governor, governor, and then U.S. senator from his home state of Mississippi.

Theodore Bilbo was born in a small Southern town to a poor Confederate army soldier and a mother named Obedience. He graduated from neither college nor law school, but passed the bar and hung out his shingle in Poplarville, Mississippi in 1907. His first problem had already reared its head by then: Bilbo had been teaching on the side while working on his studies, but was dismissed when he was accused of seducing a student.

Bilbo's early days in the world of politics didn't start off any better. Just two years into his state senate career, he accepted a bribe of $645 to throw his vote to a candidate for a special U.S. Senate election. Bilbo admitted to taking the money, but claimed he did it just in order to prove that bribes were being offered. He was put in the dock and nearly expelled; the Senate resolution called him "unfit to sit with honest, upright men in a respectable legislative body." Yet somehow, Bilbo managed to hold on to his seat.

Next, Bilbo set his sights on the lieutenant governor's office, but his campaign wouldn't be without incident. His mouth had gotten the better of him before, and it would again. After Bilbo called Civil War veteran Washington Gibbs a "renegade Confederate soldier," the affronted Gibbs beat Bilbo up with a cane. Then, after Bilbo called political opponent J. J. Henry "a cross between a hyena and a mongrel . . . suckled by a sow and educated by a fool," Henry tracked Bilbo down and smacked him around with the butt of a pistol. Yet when all was said and done, Theodore Bilbo's campaign was a success; he took his spot as lieutenant governor and went on to win the governorship in 1915.

Many politicians have their scandals, big or small, but Theodore Bilbo certainly managed to get into more than his fair share of crazy situations. After he was called to testify in the sexual harassment case of his lieutenant governor, Lee M. Russell, Bilbo refused to show up in court and hid out in a barn instead. After he was arrested and imprisoned for thirty days for contempt, he announced his decision to run again for governor of Mississippi from his jail cell. Perhaps not the best idea. He lost that bid in 1923, but, by 1927, he was reelected to a second term. Those who loved him stood by him.

As governor, Bilbo did indeed do some good. He created a highway commission, he appropriated more money for education than ever before, he built hospitals, and he instituted a board of bank examiners. Still, Crazy Bilbo kept rearing his ugly head.

In 1934, Bilbo won a Mississippi U.S. Senate seat, which he managed to hold on to until his death. These years were fraught with racist episodes during a time when the South was slowly changing, but Bilbo refused to evolve with the times. In 1938, he proposed legislation to "return" black American citizens to Africa. "It is essential to the perpetuation of our Anglo-Saxon civilization that white supremacy be maintained," he proclaimed, "and to maintain our civilization there is only one solution, and that is either by segregation within the United States, or by the deportation of the entire Negro race to its native heath, Africa." The proposal never made it to the Senate floor. The Democrats weren't exactly proud to call Theodore Bilbo one of their own, and they tried to keep him in check by placing him on the most innocuous committees possible, including one tasked with the question of governance for the District of Columbia. But Bilbo could not be contained.

In 1946, Theodore Bilbo went on *Meet the Press* (then a radio program) and blithely spoke about being a member of the Ku Klux Klan. "No man can leave the Klan. He takes an oath not to do that," he declared on air. "Once a Ku Klux, always a Ku Klux." His racism again reared its head again later that year in response to Etoy Fletcher.

Fletcher, a black veteran of World War II, had gone to register to vote at his town courthouse. He was refused and thrown out by town employees. He was subsequently kidnapped by four white men who took him into the woods, stripped him of his clothes, beat him with a wire, and warned him to never attempt to register as a voter again. When the news of the assault got out, Senator Bilbo got on the radio and essentially applauded the men's actions. He asked "every red-blooded Anglo-Saxon man in Mississippi to resort to any means to keep hundreds of Negroes from the polls in the July 2 primary." Bilbo left no doubt about how he meant that to be accomplished, going on to say that the most effective way to keep a black man from voting "was to see him the night before."

By then, Congress had had enough of Theodore Bilbo. They'd already been suspicious about some shady dealings with war contractors, including what looked like bribes to the tune of over $75,000, including a Cadillac and a swimming pool for his home. His comments regarding the Etoy Fletcher incident and his views on voter registration, the KKK, and other civil rights violations were the last straw. When, unbelievably, Bilbo once again won his senate race, Idaho Senator Glen H. Taylor put forth a motion that Bilbo be denied his seat.

The issue turned out to be moot. Theodore Bilbo had oral cancer (the karmic implications did not go unnoticed) and he adjourned to Poplarville, where he set about writing his racial treatise, *Take Your Choice: Separation or Mongrelization*, which he published himself. He died in the summer of 1947, before he ever returned to Washington.

EARL BUTZ

(1909–2008)

H e was a farm boy made good, and he changed forever the way American farmers worked their land. But Earl Butz was his own worst enemy.

Butz was born in Indiana on July 3, 1909, grew up on his father's farm, went off to college at Purdue University to study agriculture, and never looked back. He went on to get his Ph.D. in agricultural economics in 1937, and married his childhood sweetheart, a girl he'd met at a 4-H camp. He held several executive positions in the agriculture industry before being appointed assistant secretary of agriculture by President Eisenhower in 1948. In 1971, he was given the cabinet post of secretary of agriculture by Richard M. Nixon.

Secretary Butz's ideas on farming were far from being universally popular. He did away with President Franklin Roosevelt's New Deal policies, such as paying farmers to let their fields lie fallow when the country overproduced a certain crop and prices began to fall. FDR had remembered the Dust Bowl and the consequences of land being overplanted. But Earl Butz's goal was industrial agriculture, and he insisted that the opportunities for selling crops overseas were limitless. His mantra to farmers was, "Get big or get out." He was controversial—but aside from that, he was also a bigot.

Even as recently as the 1970s, it was not unusual to get away with remarks that were misogynistic, racist, sexist, and more, and Butz was one of those old-school politicians who didn't care about being politically correct. He had a reputation for being bawdy, and loved showing off the wood carving of fornicating elephants he kept in his office. He was also quoted publicly disparaging the "low level of economic intelligence" of America's housewives. Butz had historically seen little blowback for such behavior, but the world was changing, and Butz wasn't changing with the evolving social mores around him.

A comment he made in 1974 at the World Food Conference in Rome nearly brought about his demise. While discussing Pope Paul VI's position on birth control and how a change in Church teachings would reduce world food problems, he joked about the Pope and the Church's stand on celibacy for priests in a fake Italian accent: "He no play-a the game, he no make-a the rules." Catholics all over the world were soon up in arms, and both the Archdiocese of New York and the White House demanded that he apologize. Butz did, insisting that his remark was taken out of context.

But he had hardly learned his lesson, and again opened his big mouth in 1976, on a plane with Sonny Bono, politically conservative singer Pat Boone, and disgraced White House lawyer John Dean. The talk turned to African Americans and their politics. "I'll tell you what the coloreds want," brayed Butz. "It's three things: first, a tight pussy; second, loose shoes; and third, a warm place to shit." John Dean was writing an article for *Rolling Stone* about the 1976 Republican National Convention, and he used the line in his piece. Though he attributed it to an unnamed Cabinet member, it didn't take long for a reporter from *New Times* magazine to uncover the truth through travel logs. Even the *Washington Post* noted that anyone with knowledge of Washington politics would "have not the tiniest doubt in your mind as to which cabinet officer" would say such a horrendous thing. The line was so offensive that *Time* magazine and several other media outlets would not print his actual statement when reporting on the resulting scandal.

Earl Butz resigned on October 4, 1976, a month before the national election, and managed to stay afloat during the following years with speaking engagements and by serving as dean emeritus at his alma mater's school of agriculture. But the drama was far from over. In 1981, he pleaded guilty to tax fraud and was sentenced to five years in jail—only thirty days of which he ultimately ended up serving.

In defiance of the adage that "only the good die young," Earl Butz passed away in his sleep on February 2, 2008, at the age of 98.

CORNELIA GENEVIEVE GJESDAHL

(1912–1996)

ornelia Genevieve Gjesdahl was not your ordinary
Depression-era farm girl.

"Coya," as she was called, grew up in Minnesota with
big dreams: she wanted to be an opera singer. She pursued that
dream, leaving home and attending New York City's famed
Juilliard School. But after a year, Coya realized she didn't have
what it took, so she returned home and got married. For most
women of that era, a move to the big city and a chance at a
career would have been adventure enough, and a return to the
farm would have been the end of the story. But not for Coya.

Though she continued singing at local fairs and taught
music at schools as a side gig, Coya spent her days running a
hotel with her husband, Andy Knutson. Their marriage was

not a happy one; Andy was a drunk, and he beat Coya. But two things happened in 1948 that changed her life dramatically: the Knutsons adopted an eight-year-old son, Terry, and Coya got involved in local politics.

Coya's father was political—he was a dyed-in-the-wool socialist—so it was no surprise when she became interested in the Democratic-Farmer-Labor Party. In 1948, she became chair of the county committee, and she served as a delegate at the Democratic Convention the same year. In 1950, the DFL asked her to run for the state legislature. She did—and she won. Coya had caught the political bug, and what she wanted next was to go to Congress.

Her campaign was an uphill battle. Not only was she running against an endorsed candidate in the primary, which angered the local party leaders, but she was a woman, she was loud, she had a thick accent, and she had no money for her campaign. What Coya did have was a deep understanding of what it was like to be a Midwestern farmer. She and her son Terry—who was by then 14—worked their way across the state, sleeping in their car, arriving at farms so early in the morning that she would help the farmers milk their cows while she spoke to them about their needs and the changes they wanted to see. They didn't care that she was a woman; they cared that she understood them. Coya won the primary and, to the surprise of many, she went on to win the general election. Speaker of the House Sam Rayburn, thrilled that she had helped return Congress to the Democrats, told Coya she could choose whatever committee she wanted to sit on. Naturally, Coya chose the Agriculture Committee.

But soon all Knutson had worked to overcome was in danger when, once again, she didn't adhere to party wishes. While party bigwigs had decided to back Adlai Stevenson in his 1956 presidential bid, Coya supported Tennessee governor Estes Kefauver, with whom she shared many viewpoints about agricultural policy. Efforts from the DFL party chairman to get her in line were ignored and, in part because of Coya's generous support, Kefauver swept the Minnesota primary. The DFL leaders were upset, to say the least.

By 1958, Coya was spending most of her time with Terry in Washington, D.C. Ostensibly, she was there for political duties, but it was clear that she was also glad to be free of her husband's abuse. When rumors began suddenly sprouting up that Coya was having an affair with her chief of staff, Bill Kjeldahl, she believed they may have been started by DFL leaders, who were hungry for revenge.

Then came the letter. Its origins were suspect from the beginning, but it was signed by Andy Knutson and it was sent to a slew of reporters. Newspapers nationwide ran it with the headline, COYA, COME HOME. It read, in part:

> Coya, I want you to tell the people of the 9th District this Sunday that you are through in politics. That you want to go home and make a home for your husband and son. As your husband I compel you to do this. I'm tired of being torn apart from my family. I'm sick and tired of having you run around with other men all the time and not your husband. I love you, honey.

The author of the letter was never proven, but it appeared to be engineered by the DFL. It likely accomplished what was intended: Knutson lost her 1958 reelection bid by some thirteen hundred votes, and she failed again to regain her seat in 1960. Coya hadn't lost the bug, though; she returned to Washington and worked for many years at the Department of Defense. She attempted a congressional run again in 1977, but to no avail.

Naysayers will point out that Knutson passed no bills in her short time as a congresswoman, but she is still remembered for making great strides working on a federal student loan program, school lunch legislation, and research for cystic fibrosis. She was a true trailblazer: the state of Minnesota wouldn't elect another woman to Congress until 2000.

JOHN V. BRIGGS

(1930–)

John V. Briggs was just the kind of all-American guy you'd find in an old B movie. Raised by a single mother, he served in the United States Air Force during the Korean War, and then went on to the Naval Reserve. He even met his wife at a USO dance. A conservative Republican, Briggs was active in the Rotary Club and the local Boys and Girls Club, and, in 1966, he entered state politics as an assemblyman from Orange County, California. By 1976, after several terms as an assemblyman, the ambitious Briggs was elected to the state senate. He appeared to be a real stand-up guy with a bright political future ahead. Senator Briggs had been in the insurance business earlier in his career, and so insurance reform was one issue to which he was devoted when he got to the state legislature—but he also was quickly embroiled in another cause.

The gay rights movement had been slowly gaining a foothold since the 1969 Stonewall Riots in New York City. In 1977, Miami, Florida passed an ordinance banning discrimination against gays and lesbians in the areas of housing, employment, and public accommodation. A vocal opponent of the ordinance was Anita Bryant—beauty pageant winner, singer, and orange juice spokeswoman—who had gained a tidal wave of anti-gay support for her Save Our Children movement, which pledged to keep children from being "recruited" by homosexuals. Bryant and her crusaders sought to have the ordinance repealed. John Briggs wanted to go one giant step further.

Taking a page from Bryant's movement, Briggs worked to put Proposition 6 (also known as the Briggs Initiative) on the California state ballot in 1978. Prop 6 was designed to ban gays and lesbians—and possibly those who even supported them— from working in California public schools. Briggs said of gay teachers: "Most of them are in the closet, and frankly, that's where I think they should remain." However, the ban would have included not just teachers, but administrators, counselors, and teachers' aides as well. It was the first statewide attempt to curb nascent gay rights at the voting booth.

Initially, it looked as if Briggs's campaigning on the issue was going to pay off. The Briggs Initiative gained support in its first weeks, with public opinion polls saying it had 61% of the populace on their side. Christian conservatives were beginning to grow extremely powerful, while the budding gay and lesbian rights movement found itself blindsided and unprepared.

But the gay and lesbian community worked to mobilize. San Francisco Board of Supervisors member Harvey Milk took the lead (he would be assassinated just a few weeks after the election when Prop 6 appeared on the ballot), then a legion of other politicians and activists followed. The "No on 6" campaign took hold, and people statewide were chanting, "Come out! Come out! Wherever you are!" And come out they did: the gay community and their supporters went door-to-door to educate voters on the harm Prop 6 could do. A group of gay Republican activists calling themselves the Log Cabin Republicans also organized themselves to help stave off the initiative. Governor Jerry Brown backed "No on 6." So did Jimmy Carter. And perhaps most surprising of all, Republican ex-governor Ronald Reagan spoke out—a shocking turn, considering Reagan's subsequent long silence as president on AIDS and gay rights. Reagan went on the record saying, "Whatever else it is, homosexuality is not a contagious disease like measles. Prevailing scientific opinion is that an individual's sexuality is determined at a very early age and that a child's teachers do not really influence this."

When November 7 came and went, Prop 6 was defeated 58.4% to 41.6%. John Briggs retired from the state senate in 1981. He went on to a career as a lobbyist, but was haunted by allegations of intolerance. In 2008, during a campaign for the board of directors in his 55-and-over adult community, Briggs finally commented on his past: "With the passage of over thirty years, America has changed—including me. . . . Like President Reagan, and most of the country, I think differently now, and have put aside the '70s and '80s, and respectfully request others do as well and move on to the civil side of life."

DAVID ERNEST DUKE

(1950–)

D avid Duke is the perfect example of how to commit political suicide—over and over and over again. Rarely has one candidate run so much and won so little.

To look at David Duke's list of unsuccessful campaigns, it would be laughable if it weren't so frightening. He began his very lengthy string of losses in 1975 as a Democrat from Louisiana, vying for a seat in the state senate. He failed and tried again in 1979, in a different district, with no luck then either.

In the 1980s and early '90s, Duke entered political races like they were buffet lines. Between 1988 and 1992, he ran in five elections—one every year for five years: a bid for president of the United States in 1988; a congressional seat in Louisiana in 1989; a Louisiana U.S. senate seat in 1990; governor of Louisiana in 1991; back to running for president in 1992.

He did win one race: the 1989 special election for a Louisiana House seat to replace someone who had received a judicial appointment. Duke ran as a Republican, and, from that point on, the rest of his efforts to gain office would be as a GOP contender. Duke's win was a squeaker: he pulled 8,459 votes to his opponent's 8,232. His term was fairly undistinguished. During the 1990s, Duke ran in various races in Louisiana and on the national scene; in some races, the Republican Party went so far as to attempt to block his campaigns.

However, Duke's reputation as the "constant campaigner" is a mere sideline compared to how he devoted the rest of his time. He had joined the Ku Klux Klan back in 1967 and started making waves while in college in the early 1970s, going so far as to have parties on the date of Hitler's birthday and dressing up in a Nazi uniform on campus. In 1975, Duke founded the Knights of the Ku Klux Klan (KKKK) and deemed himself its Grand Wizard. The group toned down the old, extremely outspoken racist language and instead concentrated on talking about the "love of the white race."

To that end, Duke started the National Association for the Advancement of White People in 1979, and later rolled it into a shiny new version of white supremacism in 2000 with the debut of European-American Unity and Rights Organization (EURO). Their core values are racially pointed, if not explicit: EURO is intent on ending affirmative action, repealing hate crime legislation, preserving white heritage, and passing strict immigration laws. "I have the same vision I think the Founding Fathers of this country had," Duke has said of his organization.

Throughout his career, Duke has been accused of unsavory behavior on the campaign trail: stealing mailing lists, working fundraising scams, and absconding with money earmarked for other uses. Neither was the government convinced that Duke's finances were on the up-and-up, either. In 2002, Duke pleaded guilty to filing false tax returns and to a mail fraud scam that was described by the *New York Times* in no uncertain terms: "Mr. Duke was accused of telling supporters that he was in financial straits, then misusing the money they sent him from 1993 to 1999 . . . us[ing] the money for personal investments and gambling trips." It sent him to jail for over a year.

Following his legal woes, Duke moved his home base to Europe and earned a doctoral degree in the Ukraine at a university that has been called "one of the most persistent anti-Semitic institutions in Eastern Europe" by the U.S. State Department. (He now consistently refers to himself as "Dr. Duke" on his website and to the press.) The emphasis of Duke's work has turned noticeably anti-Semitic since the millennium; he insists that "the Jews are trying to destroy all other cultures—as a survival mechanism—the only Nazi country in the world is Israel." In 2009, he was arrested in the Czech Republic on the suspicion of "promotion of movements seeking suppression of human rights" while there to promote his book, *My Awakening: A Path to Racial Understanding*, a study of his thoughts on racial separatism, with a lecture at a neo-Nazi group. The police released him on April 23, 2009, on the agreement that he would leave the country by midnight that same day.

Today, Duke still speaks and visits in the United States, where he seems to have stopped running for office . . . for the time being.

CONSPIRACY, BRIBERY & FRAUD

If it weren't so disgusting, you'd called it ingenious. The myriad ways politicians have found to take everything they can from the people who trust them the most seems to be a lesson never learned—and a talent that's constantly evolving. There have been scams and rewards with the likes of releases for convicts, postage stamps, and fur coats. And as far as some of our elected officials seem to think, there's always room for new ideas.

EUGENE EDWARD SCHMITZ
(1864–1928)

He seemed an unlikely mayor, and in the end, he wasn't a very good one.

Eugene Schmitz played the violin for a living and went on to be a conductor, which eventually brought him to the position of president of the musicians' union in San Francisco at the end of the nineteenth century. But soon his collusion with a brainy lawyer and local political boss Abe Ruef brought about a firestorm that rivaled the approaching earthquake that would bring the City by the Bay to its knees.

Schmitz's job as union president brought him in contact with Ruef, who had been hanging about with the Republican Party bigwigs in town, waiting to grab some power. When that didn't work out, Ruef joined the new Union Labor Party instead, which brought him in contact with "Handsome Gene" Schmitz. From all reports, Abe Ruef was a comer from the get-go: he entered college at Berkeley at only fourteen years old, and went on to law school four years later at age eighteen. Ironically, Ruef's student days were filled with dreams of stamping out corruption in politics. But that's not how things turned out.

When Ruef met Schmitz, he saw the musician as a perfect candidate for San Francisco's next mayor, and Ruef set about working the campaign like gangbusters. In 1901, Schmitz won on his first bid, and the partnership set sail. Together, they devised ways to bilk and bribe people and businesses all over the city. One of their schemes was a bait-and-switch they pulled on French restaurants that were fronts for brothels; they'd promise to procure licenses for the joints and then would collect bribes to line both of their pockets. Graft was the name of the game, and Ruef and Schmitz were winning it hands down. Later, the *New York Times* would look back: "It was not long before everyone knew that while Schmitz, the fiddler, was Mayor, Abe Ruef, the lawyer, was making all the music about City Hall."

Nevertheless, when elections rolled around again in 1905, Eugene Schmitz was voted in as mayor once more. But the skullduggery at City Hall was not going unnoticed: investigations were underway. Newspaperman Fremont Older was determined to bring Schmitz and Ruef down, and he spearheaded the inquiry about the graft that permeated the city. He went to Washington, met with President Theodore Roosevelt, and convinced Roosevelt to loan out a special prosecutor and a Secret Service agent for the investigation. The president agreed, with his only caveat being that Older had to find the money to fund the investigation. The newshound enlisted the help of friend Rudolph Spreckels to help pick up the tab.

Fremont Older literally took his life in his hands leading the charge. It turned out that a number of prominent San Francisco residents were in it up to their eyeballs with Schmitz and Ruef, and though history has not revealed who exactly was behind the threats and trouble, Older and his wife were the targets of a plot to blow them up, and Fremont Older ended up being kidnapped in broad daylight on Van Ness Avenue, shoved in a car, and forced onto a train. Older's life was only spared when another passenger overheard the kidnapper's plot to do away with him and reported it to police; Older was rescued at the next station.

But just when the wheels started to turn on digging up the corruption, San Francisco's devastating earthquake hit on the morning of April 18, 1906, and Schmitz and Ruef were temporarily forgotten in the attempts to get the city back on its feet. When the investigations resumed in full force, they were in trouble deep. In November, indictments were finally handed down on both Schmitz and Ruef in the form of twenty-seven counts of graft and bribery. Ruef defiantly turned his back to the judge while the charges were read.

Ruef wasn't much help to his old pal after that. Whereas Schmitz decided to go to trial, Ruef gave it up and pleaded guilty, pointing the finger at the mayor and describing their practice of splitting bribes down the middle. Schmitz was forced out of office on June 13, 1907, but fortune smiled on him big time when it was later discovered that the indictments against him neglected to use his official title as mayor. The technicality meant he was off the hook completely, but Abe Ruef was off to San Quentin.

Eugene Schmitz went on to beat another bribery charging in 1912, which apparently convinced him there was still a clear path to City Hall. He ran for mayor of San Francisco again in 1915 and 1919, and to no one's surprise (but his own), was defeated, though he did manage to find a seat on the San Francisco Board of Supervisors in 1921.

Abe Ruef's future, however, held some unexpected surprises. Fremont Older, Ruef's former nemesis, had second thoughts: he now believed that there may have been some anti-Semitic bias involved in the punishment of Ruef, who was Jewish. The newspaper editor lobbied on Ruef's behalf for his release, even going so far as to pay Ruef to write a serialized account of his memoirs in his own newspaper, the *San Francisco Bulletin*. God Bless America; it's amazing how forgiving the public can be.

MA & PA FERGUSON

JAMES EDWARD FERGUSON
(1871–1944)

MIRIAM A. FERGUSON
(1875–1961)

I f you thought the Clinton husband-and-wife political
machine is a novelty, think again: James and Miriam Ferguson of Texas had them beat by about seventy-five years.

James Ferguson grew up in Bell County, the son of
a farmer. James helped on the farm and went to school,
though by the time he was fifteen, he'd been thrown out for

consistently bad behavior. He left home, traveled around the West working various jobs, then came back home to Texas, where he studied the law a bit. There are reports that Ferguson received his law degree without ever being tested, compliments of a family friend who sat on the bar exam committee. (Perhaps the first step in a life of misrepresentation for Jim Ferguson.) In 1899, he married Miriam A. Wallace, and one of America's most notorious political partnerships began.

Jim Ferguson started out as a small-town city attorney in Belton, Texas, and then worked as a banker for several years. Then, in 1914, the Ferguson era began, as Jim was elected governor of Texas in his first foray into politics as a Democrat and anti-prohibitionist. Though he had no prior experience as an elected official, Ferguson had worked on several campaigns, and Texans found him a savvy and personable feature on the political landscape. As a candidate, he won over the farmers by standing up for agricultural issues. So things went fairly smoothly during Governor Ferguson's first term, and he was reelected in 1916, though by then rumors of malfeasance had begun. In response to the allegations, the governor admitted that he had used state monies for personal groceries for his family, but nothing more.

Soon into his second term, Governor Jim Ferguson locked horns with the University of Texas. He wanted several faculty members let go, including William Harding Mayes. A former opponent in the most recent gubernatorial race, Mayes owned a string of newspapers that were decidedly anti-Ferguson, and the bad press brought to the surface the many charges and accusations that had been building against him, such as misappropriation of funds, failure to enforce banking laws, receiving a bribe, and other inappropriate actions. There were twenty-one charges in all, and the Texas Senate decided to remove him from office. Though Ferguson then announced he would run for a third time, it was not to be: Governor Jim Ferguson was impeached, and thus ineligible to hold public office in the state of Texas.

So it was time to move on . . . to Mrs. Ferguson. In 1925, Jim's wife Miriam decided she would run for governor, which would make her the first woman to hold the office in Texas. Evidently there were still plenty of Ferguson lovers out there, because her campaign promise was that her husband the ex-governor would help advise her, and thus their constituents would get "two governors for the price of one." Until her run for office, Miriam— called "Ma" both for her initials, Miriam Amanda, and her relationship to her husband, who then went by "Pa"—had been a wife and mother of two daughters. She had zero political experience. Despite foes bearing banners that proclaimed "No Ma for me—too much Pa," Miriam won the election, and the team of "Ma and Pa" Ferguson was born. They really had only one political difference of opinion: she was a teetotaler, and he was all for ending Prohibition.

Ma landed in hot water pretty quickly into her first term. She had campaigned on a promise to force the Ku Klux Klan to unmask, but the bill she'd gotten through was soon over-turned in court. She also promised she'd cut state spending, but went on to increase it instead. However, the real show-stopper was her pardoning of convicts. Ma Ferguson released nearly four thousand jailbirds in her two terms as governor, amounting to about one hundred a month. Many of them had been locked up simply for breaking Prohibition laws, and

Ma said she was trying to ease an overcrowded prison system and save Texans some money. But evidence pointed to both Fergusons taking bribes of land and cash for the pardons. So, it turned out that breaking the law might have been the other thing Ma and Pa had in common.

One might think that Ma and Pa's political careers may have been over at that point. Jim Ferguson had no luck in a weak 1920 presidential bid, nor for United States Senate in 1922, and Miriam sat out the election of 1928 to let things cool off. But then Miriam was reelected in 1932, and they headed back to the governor's mansion. Though Miriam continued the convict releases, voters seem to have lost interest in calling her on the carpet, and Miriam's second term was much less controversial. After another respite from political life for both Ma and Pa, Miriam ran for governor one more time at the age of sixty-five, but lost. It would be sixty years after her stewardship of Texas until Ann Richards was elected the second woman governor of the Lone Star State.

Ma and Pa Ferguson fell prey to financial woes and lost their ranch in 1935. Jim died in 1944, and Miriam in 1961, just as another famous First Lady, Jackie Kennedy, came on the scene.

JAMES MICHAEL CURLEY

(1874–1958)

O f the many Irish-American politicians who have made a
name in the history of United States politics—whether
for being reviled or adored—perhaps the most infamous
of them all was James Michael Curley, who served four terms
as mayor of Boston, one term as governor of Massachusetts—
and two terms in jail. Curley was outspoken, rough, charis-
matic, and, from 1914 through 1950, he successfully held off
the WASPy Beacon Hill Brahmin types to keep Beantown
in the palm of his hand.

Born in 1874, Curley entered the political arena in 1898,
winning a seat on the Boston Common Council. By 1904,
Curley had his first visit to the slammer. He had agreed to
take a civil service exam for a postal worker job for a friend

who thought he wouldn't be able to pass the test; Curley was recognized at the exam and jailed for ninety days for fraud. Contrary to what one might think, the escapade made him more popular than ever. Boston was 40% Irish by then, and Curley was making a reputation for himself as a man of the people—at least, of his people. His parents had come from Ireland, and he grew up in a dirt-poor neighborhood. James Curley knew what it meant to stick together with your family and neighbors. He was running for alderman at the time, and rather than hurting his chances, his cheating and subsequent punishment helped him win in a landslide. "He did it for a friend," became the cry for Curley, and it was all voters seemed to care about.

Curley's goal in life was to help the poor and underrepresented. He did it often out of his own pocket—and often whether or not it was legal. He blew into Massachusetts politics with the attitude that the Yankee WASPs had the means and the obligation to help the poorer immigrants, who now were much of Boston's voting population. It was a breath of fresh air to some, but it made him extremely unpopular among many Bay Staters. Curley raised taxes for the elite and began public works projects like building libraries, public beaches, playgrounds, and parks. He tackled bridges, roads, subway stations, and municipal buildings. He was a New Deal kind of guy before FDR ever called it the New Deal.

But make no mistake, as Curley gave with one hand, he was always busy taking with the other. Biographer Joseph Dineen said, "Everybody knew there wasn't a contract awarded that did not carry with it a cut for Curley." Yet Curley adored being called the "Mayor of the Poor," and he believed it to be true. And the people backed him up. When he was convicted on nine counts of mail fraud in 1947 during his fourth term as mayor, and could not pay the fine of over $40,000, Bostonians chipped in to help their beloved friend. The *Chicago Tribune* reported that when he returned home from Washington following the trial, huge crowds of admirers awaited him. "Three cheers for the greatest figure in America!" shouted a fan. Curley ended up in jail, but President Truman cut his sentence short after pressure from Massachusetts politicians. In 1950, Truman gave Curley a full pardon for both the 1904 and 1947 convictions.

Like so many larger-than-life people, James Michael Curley was as loathed as he was loved. A poor immigrant, he came on like gangbusters into a Yankee stronghold and had such an effect on Boston's changing political face that it's said the Brahmins started to move to the suburbs during his long reign to escape his long political reach. "Curley gets things done," he would say, and like it or not, that was the truth. Another famous Irish-American politician, Speaker of the House Tip O'Neill, said, "The first night I sat down with Ronald Reagan in the White House, the president wanted to hear all about James Michael Curley. The same was true of Jimmy Carter, and just about every other politician I've ever known."

Curley won a lot, but not always. In 1951 and again in 1955, he made bids for an unprecedented fifth term as mayor of Boston and was defeated, having lost much of his backroom, old-school constituency, both the Irish and the considerable Yankee Democratic base he had enjoyed for decades. One only has to watch the movie *The Last Hurrah*, starring Spencer

Tracy as Boston mayor Frank Skeffington, to see the downfall of a fictional Curley come to life on the screen.

It seemed no matter how many times and in how many ways Curley committed political suicide, he was a man who knew how to rise from the dead. One of the greatest Curley stories about coming back from behind is from 1914, when he had his eye on the mayor's office for the first time. His opponent was Boston mayor John F. "Honey Fitz" Fitzgerald, JFK's grandfather. Fitzgerald, an incumbent, was aiming for a third term, while Curley was itching for his first win. There was talk around town about the married mayor's girl on the side, "Toodles" Ryan. Just leaking this tidbit to the press wouldn't be nearly enough fun for James Michael Curley. He announced that he was going to deliver a series of lectures, one of which was titled, "Great Lovers, from Cleopatra to Toodles." The incumbent quietly left the race, and Curley was in.

JIMMY WALKER

(1881–1946)

New York City mayor James "Jimmy" Walker liked a drink. And he liked a girl or two. He was a perfect man for the city in the Roaring Twenties, so frequent a visitor in the nightclubs and casinos that he became known as the "Night Mayor." Born and bred in Greenwich Village, he dressed like a dandy, glad-handed his fellow New Yorkers, and happily joined his citizenry for long afternoons at Yankee Stadium. New York loved Jimmy Walker, and Jimmy loved it back.

Lest it seem that being a gadabout was his only talent, Mayor Walker was also seriously dedicated to building a modern city. By the time he started his job in City Hall on January 1, 1926, he had well over a decade of political experience in the New York state legislature, and it showed. He knew how to get things done. Walker's tenure saw the creation of the Department of Sanitation as well as the beginning of construction work on the Triborough Bridge, the Queens–Midtown Tunnel, and the West Side Highway. He knew what the people wanted: he changed the blue laws so New Yorkers could go to the theater on Sundays, he legalized boxing, and he was anti-Prohibition (there were said to be 32,000 speakeasies in the city when Walker took office). He also fought to institute workman's compensation laws, eight-hour workdays for women, safeguard policies for tenements, and the preservation of the five-cent subway fare.

It was hard to hate Jimmy Walker, and the public was pretty thrilled with him during his first term. Sure, he didn't show up to his office until noon, and left his wife at home and was out with a chorus girl most nights. But he was a real man of the people. Richer than they were, but he was one of them still.

Times were good all around during Walker's first years at City Hall, and the warm feelings flowed over into the next mayoral election, when Walker beat Fiorello La Guardia soundly for another term as mayor. Jimmy Walker was getting wealthier, though, and soon enough there were questions about from whence this bounty flowed. Then, in 1929, the stock market crash kicked off the beginning of the Great Depression. Walker's personal finances took a huge hit, and New York's Cardinal Archbishop Hayes put the mayor in his sights as an example of the kind of behavior and morals that were bringing the nation to its knees. Both Cardinal Hayes and Jimmy Walker had powerful ties to the Tammany Hall

Democratic machine that virtually controlled New York politics at the time, and Tammany began to see that Walker was
becoming more of a liability than an asset. It seemed better to
side with the Church than with Jimmy Walker.

Soon Mayor Walker had both church and state against
him. In 1930, the Hofstadter Committee was organized by
the New York State Legislature to investigate corruption in
New York City, in particular the wrongdoings in the police
department and the magistrate's courts. The group was
headed by Judge Samuel Seabury (and would become also
known as the Seabury Commission), and their diligent work
brought more than one thousand witnesses before the Commission to tell their part in an appalling tale of corruption.
The main scam going down was arresting people—generally
prostitutes—and giving them the option to pay up or go to
the slammer. One vice cop told the Commission he would
walk up and down Broadway, simply arresting women. He
made over twelve hundred vice arrests in a decade, and his
bank account showed it: his $3,000-a-year patrolman's salary
belied the $30,500 he stashed away in only two years. Another
sheriff with an $8,000-a-year job had a managed to set aside
a $400,000 nest egg after six years on the job. The system
was rotten, and everybody was getting paid off: cops, judges,
bailiffs, lawyers—everybody got a piece.

Jimmy Walker had been able to steer clear of the courtroom so far, but the death of Vivian Gordon changed that.
Gordon was a prostitute with a heart of coal. She would frequently blackmail rich customers by threatening to reveal their
infidelities to their wives. It was a good living. But Gordon
had one pressing problem. She had lost custody of her daughter

to her ex-husband after she was arrested for prostitution. She began to suspect that her husband and a dirty cop had conspired to put her in jail so that she would lose her daughter. She decided she would testify before the Seabury Commission in the hope of getting her child back. Five days after her court appearance, Vivian Gordon was found strangled. Governor Franklin D. Roosevelt decided that the Seabury Commission had to dig deeper. New York City was riding roughshod over the law, and it was all because of Jimmy Walker.

Judge Seabury was advised not to look directly into Jimmy Walker's eyes when he interrogated him—that's how magnetic Walker's Irish charm was purported to be. But the records didn't lie. When the commission looked into Mayor Walker's finances, they found money and accounts that just shouldn't have been there. There was even a slush fund just for "Our Jimmy" (as New Yorkers called him), to which businessmen and politicians "donated" in return for favors. Something was obviously amiss, and New Yorkers were beginning to make the connection—whether right or wrong—that Jimmy Walker himself was responsible for Vivian Gordon's death.

Roosevelt strong-armed Walker, asking for his resignation in 1932. Walker conceded, took his famous chorus girl, Betty Compton, and got on a ship to Europe. They married, and eventually returned to the United States where Jimmy returned to his second love, music. He ran Majestic Records for a time and even wrote a few popular tunes of the day, the most memorable being, "Will You Love Me in December (As You Do in May)?" He even got a job from his former political nemesis, Fiorello La Guardia (by then mayor himself), who gave Walker a gig as municipal arbiter to the garment industry in 1940.

Columnist Ben Hecht once said of Walker, "No man could hold life so carelessly without falling down a manhole before he is done." That may be true, but Walker biographer Gene Fowler said it even better when he said that Jimmy "wore New York in his lapel like a boutonniere."

Now, that's Our Jimmy.

WILLIAM LANGER

(1886–1959)

T alk about a terrible first day on the job. When William Langer showed up to be sworn in as United States senator from North Dakota on January 1, 1941, he was told that the senate majority leader, Alben Barkley, had a complaint to address. It turned out that some concerned citizens from Langer's home state had filed accusations of bribery, kickbacks, charging for false services, and plenty more. Many of the sitting senators felt such allegations were not befitting a new man on the job. They did not want to allow William Langer into the Senate.

This was not Langer's first legal wrangle. After studying law at Columbia University, he passed up a career with a white-shoe firm in New York City to head back to home ground. He was elected North Dakota's attorney general in

1916 and then, in 1932, he became North Dakota's governor. That's when his serious troubles began. In an odd but completely legal financial move, Governor Langer required every state employee to "donate" 5% of their salary to his pro-farmer party, the Nonpartisan League Republicans. The policy was above board, but when it was discovered that federal monies were coming into the governor's office, that was not okay with the United States government. After a monthlong trial, Langer was found guilty in 1934 of misuse of federal funds and sentenced to eighteen months in prison and a fine of $10,000.

It was no surprise, then, that the North Dakota Supreme Court ordered Governor Langer removed from office, citing him as a convicted felon. Langer had a better idea: he holed himself up with a few friends in the governor's mansion, declared martial law, and drew up a new declaration of independence. The governor decided that if North Dakota seceded from the United States, he would still be running the seceded territory. He initially insisted that the United States Supreme Court hear him out, but he eventually relented and was forced to step down (and to leave the mansion).

Due to one crazy mishap after another, the state went through three governors in seven months. (Even Lydia Langer, William's wife, ran and lost in 1934.) Meanwhile, William Langer was navigating through a maze of trials and appeals, and he eventually got an overturned conviction. He ran again for governor and was back in the state capital by the beginning of 1937.

After a full two-year term without any legal interruption, Langer set his sights on the United States Senate and won the seat on his second try, bringing us back to that fateful 1941 date when he showed up in Washington, D.C. to start his new job. The Senate did finally agree to seat him, but an inquiry into past irregularities as governor took up the entirety of the following year. The Committee on Privileges and Elections finally handed over a more than 4,000-page report, concluding that Langer was morally unfit to hold his Senate seat. The rub on a decision like this, of course, is that North Dakotans had already made their own choice at the polls, a choice which the minority members on the committee stressed. Langer sat in the Senate chamber while this moral debate swirled around him, but he came out of it on top: a majority ruled that he could stay. His constituents agreed, electing him to three more terms.

"Wild Bill" Langer certainly had a roller coaster ride of a career, and it was strewn with other oddities as well. He was such a strict isolationist that he was one of only two senators who voted against the United Nations. And in 1945, when Red-baiting really started to heat up, Langer went after the beloved "Little Tramp" himself, Charlie Chaplin. The comedian and filmmaker was a lefty, and many in Washington were suspicious as to why the English-born Chaplin had never applied for United States citizenship. Senator Langer introduced a bill in the Senate to have the attorney general's office investigate Chaplin, with an eye toward deportation. (The bill didn't pass.) In 1950, Langer filibustered on the veto of a Communist registration bill for an impressive 29 hours and 53 minutes, until he collapsed on the Senate floor.

William Langer managed to stay in the Senate until 1959. He was still so popular with voters that even though he would not leave his sick wife's bedside during his last election—made not a single speech nor earned the party endorsement—he still won his final race in 1958.

J. PARNELL THOMAS

(1895–1970)

There is not much that is more satisfying than when the mighty fall, especially when they have spent their life in the pursuit of others' ruination. And the fall of J. Parnell Thomas made many people happy.

Born in Jersey City in 1895, he was a man with his sights set high. Believing an Irish background could limit his future, he changed his name (from John Parnell Feeney Jr. to John Parnell Thomas) and then his religion (from Roman Catholic to Episcopalian). He got himself an Ivy League education, did a stint in the army, and headed into the banking business in Manhattan for nearly two decades. Then he got the political bug. He became mayor of his small town in New Jersey, then state assemblyman. In 1937, he entered Congress, where he remained until his resignation in 1950. It was in those last three years that he really did the damage, as the chair of the House Un-American Activities Committee (HUAC), which had been formed in 1938 to investigate allegations of Communist activity in the United States even before the Cold War.

Though HUAC had been active for more than a decade by that point, Thomas's years at the helm were perhaps the most high profile and the most frightening. The second "Red Scare" (the first had been after World War I) had America in its grip, and anything or anyone that seemed even vaguely suspicious went under the microscope. Thomas decided to take on Hollywood, which he was certain was chock-full of Communists and left-wing propagandists. He found allies in the Motion Picture Alliance for the Preservation of American Ideals, formed during World War II by conservative Hollywood headliners including Walt Disney, Ronald Reagan, Barbara Stanwyck, John Wayne, Cecil B. DeMille, and Clark Gable. Writer Ayn Rand penned a pamphlet for the MPAPAI, which read in part:

> The purpose of the Communists in Hollywood is *not* the production of political movies openly advocating Communism. Their purpose is *to corrupt our moral premises by corrupting non-political movies*—by introducing small, casual bits of propaganda into innocent stories—thus making people absorb the basic principles of Collectivism *by indirection and implication.*

While Rand and many other members were called before HUAC as friendly witnesses, it was, of course, the Hollywood Ten that made the real news and are remembered by history as the victims of the abominable witch hunt undertaken by the committee. Alvah Bessie, Herbert Biberman, Lester Cole, Edward Dmytryk, Ring Lardner, Jr. John Howard Lawson, Albert Maltz, Samuel Ornitz, Adrian Scott, and Dalton Trumbo were all brought before Thomas's committee in the fall of 1947 to testify, because they were believed to have Communist affiliations. When they called upon their First Amendment rights to free speech and assembly, they were all cited for contempt of Congress and served a year in prison. But that was hardly their only punishment. They were all blacklisted by the Hollywood studios and most never got work again—at least not under their own names.

Much as the American public had become frightened by an impending Russian threat, they now began to fear the ferocity of the trials. That question—"Are you or have you ever been a member of the Communist Party?"—chilled liberal citizens to the bone. Screenwriters, directors, and producers weren't the only ones who had gone to a meeting or two in the past.

And so it's not surprising that by 1948, the witch hunt finally turned on J. Parnell Thomas. "Washington Merry-Go-Round" columnist Drew Pearson, a journalist who disapproved of Thomas's and HUAC's tactics, helped to take him down. Thomas's secretary, Helen Campbell, cinched Person's investigation when she began to send him information on Thomas's illegal activities. It turned out that he had been putting friends and no-show employees on his payroll for years and depositing the money into his own account.

In the courtroom, J. Parnell Thomas called upon the Fifth Amendment, as had many of the people he brought before HUAC. He, too, was tried and convicted. He resigned from Congress in 1950 and was sent to prison for eighteen months. He was incarcerated, ironically, with Lester Cole and Ring Lardner Jr.—two members of the Hollywood Ten who he had helped put in jail.

LLEWELYN SHERMAN ADAMS

(1899–1986)

R arely is there such a mortifying way to lose your job as chief of staff for the president of the United States than over a fur coat. But that is exactly how Sherman Adams lost his.

Adams had an auspicious old New England upbringing: a descendant of Henry Adams of the presidential Adams family, he was raised in fancy East Dover, Vermont, graduated from Dartmouth College, did a bid in the marines in World War I, and then started in private business in New Hampshire. It was during his time at a paper mill that the higher-ups there encouraged him to get into politics; they knew a smart guy when they saw one, and they believed he could do a better job than the politicians in Concord were doing for them. And so, early in World War II, Adams entered politics as a Republican in the state legislature, where he also served as speaker of the House. He became a congressman in 1945 and then, after one failed attempt, Sherman Adams became governor of New Hampshire in 1949.

Adams's New England frugality shone through during his time as governor. New Hampshire was in sorry shape after World War II. Governor Adams asked for more aid and insurance for the elderly, and he reorganized state operations. He received national recognition when he served as the chair for the U.S. Conference of Governors. After being one of the few governors who supported Dwight D. Eisenhower for president in 1952, he was asked by Ike to act as his campaign manager. Thus began Adams's all-powerful political embrace of the future 34th president of the United States.

The role was technically "assistant to the president," but Adams began using "chief of staff" in a nod to Eisenhower's military background, and it stuck. From the beginning, Adams didn't make friends; he allowed only Cabinet members and a few others easy access to the commander-in-chief. Anybody else went through the new chief of staff—and getting through wasn't easy. Adams kept such a tight rein on Eisenhower's world that Washington wags began to call him the "Abominable No-Man." The thing was, it all suited Ike perfectly, so the wall around him stood firm. Adams ran staff meetings and reportedly made all but the most top-level White House decisions. It seemed that he liked it that way too. The joke around town (and it was funny because it was true) was that two Democrats met on the street, and one said, "Gee, wouldn't it be terrible if Eisenhower died and Nixon became president?" And the other one says, "Wouldn't it be terrible if Sherman Adams died and Eisenhower became president?"

Ike trusted his chief of staff implicitly, and for a long time he had reason to do so. For five years, things ran smoothly. But then there were whispers that Sherman Adams had interfered with a Civil Aeronautics Board decision about closing a faltering airline. That particular investigation into Adams's involvement went nowhere, but the House Special Subcommittee on Legislative Oversight now had him in its sights.

And then Bernard Goldfine, a longtime Adams buddy from Boston, came into the picture. Goldfine owned a textile mill and had been charged with mislabeling fabric; it appeared that Goldfine's textile was made more of synthetic nylon and less of the luxurious vicuña wool (an expensive fiber from a llama-like South American animal) than he promised. Word on the street was that once the Federal Trade Commission had started sniffing around the mislabeling, he had called his old pal Adams to look into the investigation. The chief of staff had reportedly called the FTC chairman about the investigation. Had Adams actually procured favors that were unseemly (and possibly illegal) from such a high-ranking government official? Adams confessed that he may have had some conversations with government officials, but that he never attempted to exert any influence on Bernard Goldfine's behalf. But the evidence seemed to prove otherwise.

The evidence all came back to that the glorious vicuña— but this time in the form of a coat. It was alleged that Goldfine had gifted Adams an Oriental rug, a few Boston hotel stays, and an expensive vicuña coat. The chief of staff managed to explain them all away fairly convincingly to the House Special

Subcommittee on Legislative Oversight. The hotel room was already owned by Goldfine; the rug had been so old it had to be tossed, Adams said. But Oh!, that beautiful coat. There was no excuse for that.

Adams couldn't seem to talk his way out of this one, and people were clamoring for him to step down—even his fellow Republicans, who feared the hullabaloo would hurt their chances in the 1960 presidential election. Eisenhower (and, it must be said, Vice President Richard Nixon, whom Adams had counseled during his "Checkers speech" about his own financial improprieties) stuck by his side. "I need him," Ike said simply.

Ultimately, the pressure grew too great. Adams did resign, at Eisenhower's request, on September 22, 1958, in a radio broadcast in which he said he was the victim of "a campaign of vilification." In his 1961 memoir, *Firsthand Report: The Story of the Eisenhower Administration*, Adams would clarify the Goldfine incident: "I never intended to do anything for him. But I did not stop to consider that in making a personal call or an inquiry concerning a matter in which he was involved, I might be giving the officials in the Federal agency the erroneous impression that I had a personal interest in their ruling or decision."

Following his resignation, Sherman Adams returned to New Hampshire and opened a very successful ski business at Loon Mountain, which has perhaps become his finest legacy.

THE MITCHELLS

JOHN N. MITCHELL
(1913–1988)

MARTHA MITCHELL
(1918–1976)

I t seemed throughout John Mitchell's storied career, if it
wasn't one thing, it was another. He enjoyed a lucrative
livelihood as a municipal bond lawyer for thirty years in
New York City and perhaps should have left it at that. But law
firm pal Richard Nixon recruited him to run his successful
(at last) 1968 presidential campaign—and the prize was a job

as United States attorney general. Mitchell kept that position until 1972, when he returned as campaign manager for Nixon's reelection. This afforded him another title: director of the Committee to Re-elect the President, a group which was soon enough acronym-ized as CREEP all over the national news. The Committee was officially charged with fundraising for Nixon's run; unofficially, it was involved in money laundering schemes and the creation of slush funds that were eventually used to try and bury the Watergate break-in on June 17, 1972.

Mitchell was questioned by the *Washington Post*'s Carl Bernstein in 1972 about the CREEP slush fund money being under his aegis. When he was asked specifically whether it was used for spying on the Democrats, Mitchell reportedly snapped, "Katie Graham's [then the *Post*'s publisher] gonna get her tit caught in a big fat wringer if that's published." It did hit the papers, of course, and Mitchell turned out to be one of many charged for the Watergate break-ins and the ensuing scandal. He was found guilty and served nineteen months in prison for conspiracy, perjury, and obstruction of justice.

But John wasn't the only Mitchell making headlines during the scandal. Always in the background there was Martha, Mitchell's second wife and quite regularly the thorn in his political side. As the Watergate hubbub was heating up, Martha—who, it seemed, liked to drink a bit—began to call reporters, complaining about Nixon and hinting at dastardly deeds in our nation's capital. "I'm not going to stand for all of those dirty things that go on," she told journalist Helen Thomas. Martha Mitchell was anathema in Washington, but the rest of America just could not wait to hear what the "Mouth of the South" had to say next. The height of

Marthamania came when she insisted she had been held captive in a California hotel room and drugged to keep her silent. Though the veracity of that incident may remain in question, the claim—coupled with her other allegations, which turned out to be accurate—brought about the origin of what the psychiatric community still calls the "Martha Mitchell effect." In such cases, mental health experts misdiagnose a patient because they perceive the patient's perception of real events to be delusional, when they are, in fact, entirely true.

John Mitchell left Martha in 1973. She later fumed that he had taken the maid, their chauffeur and, most importantly, their Rolodex of phone numbers. He later quipped when sentenced to prison, "It could have been a hell of a lot of worse. They could have sentenced me to spend the rest of my life with Martha." It wouldn't have been a long sentence, though. While the former attorney general lived quietly until he died of a heart attack at seventy-five in 1988, Martha died alone at the age of fifty-seven in 1976.

She did, however, survive long enough to see Richard Nixon resign.

SPIRO T. AGNEW

(1918–1996)

Nattering nabobs of negativism!"

They were four words arranged together perhaps only once in the history of politics—but anyone who read a newspaper or watched TV in 1970 heard and snickered at this ridiculous yet unforgettable turn of phrase spoken by then–Vice President Spiro T. Agnew, Richard M. Nixon's second-in-command.

Back in the day before social media really knew how to ruin a career, Agnew was speaking about the antagonistic relationship he had with the press. The entire quote—which was even nuttier in full—was delivered to the Republican state convention in California: "In the United States today, we have more than our share of the nattering nabobs of negativism.

They have formed their own 4-H Club—the 'hopeless, hysterical hypochondriacs of history.'"

It was great stuff—sure to get some attention for the country's number one second banana. The public found it as hilarious as it was nutty. The veep—who was both the first Greek American and the first Maryland resident to attain the office—was a bit of political oddball, but he was an oddball who suddenly had the ears of America. He continually went after the anti–Vietnam War crowd with his trademark barbs, calling them "pusillanimous pussyfooters," "supercilious sophisticates," and "an effete corps of impudent snobs who characterize themselves as intellectuals." Of course, Agnew didn't write his own stuff; he had two great speechwriters who both ended up going pretty far themselves: soon-to-be top journalist William Safire and political commentator and occasional presidential candidate Pat Buchanan.

Despite talk of replacing him on the 1972 presidential ticket, Agnew had enough of a conservative base that he was kept on. Still, Nixon never had much use for Agnew. The vice president turned out to be a popular speaker and fundraiser, but Nixon never really worried about being overshadowed. "No assassin in his right mind would kill me," Nixon said, intimating the consider-the-alternative school of thought. It wouldn't be too long before Nixon found he preferred to have the vice president in the spotlight after all.

By 1973, when Watergate waters were roiling around Nixon and the president needed a scapegoat to divert attention from the super-scandal, the vice president was the perfect patsy. The U.S. attorney came at Agnew full force, investigating tax fraud, bribery, extortion, and conspiracy—all dating back to Agnew's days as county executive and then governor of Maryland. (The allegations were meant to divert attention from Watergate, after all, not sully the White House further.)

Formally charged with accepting bribes, Agnew pleaded no contest, was put on probation, and paid a $10,000 fine. (The bribery charge would be proven several years later in Maryland criminal court.) Agnew became the first vice president in United States history to resign his office due to criminal charges. But the real drama lay not in the charges, but in Agnew's resignation itself: he insisted that Nixon's chief of staff Alexander Haig threatened him. In fact, Agnew titled his 1980 memoir *Go Quietly . . . Or Else*, in a nod the words he claimed Haig said in order to prompt his resignation. Agnew wrote in his book:

> This directive was aimed at me like a gun at my head. That is the only way I can describe it. I was told, "Go quietly—or else." I feared for my life. If a decision had been made to eliminate me— through an automobile accident, a fake suicide, or whatever—the order would not have been traced back to the White House.

It was clear to Agnew: it was time to go. And go he did. He would not speak to Nixon for the rest of his life.

Gerald Ford succeeded Spiro Agnew, a very popular choice on Capitol Hill. As for Richard Nixon, he didn't manage to take enough of the heat off himself. He didn't last a year, and fell prey to scandal himself, stepping down as president on August 8, 1974. And then Gerald Ford stepped into that job, too.

BESS MYERSON

(1924–2014)

A Jewish Miss America? In the 1940s, it seemed improbable, if not impossible. And then to end up in New York City politics? Enough already!

Born in the Bronx as the daughter of Russian immigrants, Bess Myerson was a beautiful and brainy girl, with musical talent to boot, who attended New York's fledgling High School of Music & Art and then went on to Hunter College. She helped support her family by teaching piano lessons and she did a little modeling on the side. Unbeknownst to her, Myerson's sister Sylvia entered her in the 1945 Miss New York City contest. Myerson was initially annoyed, but she warmed up to the idea when she learned of the scholarship prize money. But she was far from a pageant pro;

Myerson was such a neophyte that had to borrow a bathing suit to compete.

Myerson went all the way, ending her beauty pageant sweep by winning Miss America in 1945. Throughout her road to the crown, many tried to convince her to change her name; it was so obviously Jewish, they said. The 21-year-old stood her ground, however, proud of her heritage, and the pageant lost several anti-Semitic sponsors. Myerson later said, "It was the most important decision I ever made. It told me who I was, that I was first and foremost a Jew." Myerson became a heroine, not just to young Jewish women, but to Jews everywhere. This was at the very end of World War II, and for her to speak out when the tragedies of the Holocaust were just coming to light was extraordinary.

The contest win turned out to be a mixed blessing. Myerson played the piano on the vaudeville circuit for a bit and made a little money, but she was shattered to encounter NO JEWS signs at hotels along the way. Then the Anti-Defamation League approached her about a series of lectures, and her life began to turn around. Soon a TV producer saw her speak and offered her a job on a game show. Her glamorous persona led her from being "The Lady in Mink" (an early version of Vanna White) on the game show *The Big Payoff* to substitute hosting on the *Today* show to obtaining perhaps her most famous role: as a decade-long panelist on *I've Got a Secret*.

In 1969, Myerson left the world of TV when New York mayor John V. Lindsay appointed her as the first commissioner of Department of Consumer Affairs. She was an early pioneer in consumer protection, chaired the campaign of New York's future mayor, Edward I. Koch, and served on various presidential committees. She even vied, unsuccessfully, for a New York Senate seat. Miss America had finally become an important mover and shaker—and a really classy one at that. Until, that is, the juicy tabloid fodder that became known as the "Bess Mess" surfaced.

Divorced twice and squired by many, romance came Myerson's way once more when she began dating married sewer contractor Andy Capasso. Myerson was, at the time, working as Mayor Koch's commissioner of the Department of Cultural Affairs. It was a glitzy and highbrow position that no one would ever expect to see foster a steamy sex scandal that turned into allegations of a judicial backroom deal. But that's just what happened. When Capasso's wife learned of his Miss America affair, she filed for divorce. Capasso decided his alimony payments were too much, and before you knew it, Bess was socializing with Capasso's divorce trial judge, Hortense Gabel. And then, lo and behold, the judge's daughter, Sukhreet, landed a job at Cultural Affairs with Myerson. It was all very suspicious, and bribery was immediately suspected.

The "Bess Mess" led to Myerson's resignation from her position, and it severely tainted the Koch administration. In time, Myerson, Judge Gabel, and Capasso would all be indicted on several counts by then–U.S. attorney and later New York mayor Rudolph Giuliani. All were eventually acquitted, but the damage was done as far as their careers were concerned. Capasso's troubles weren't over, though: he was eventually convicted on unrelated tax charges.

For so long, Myerson reigned as America's sweetheart; as her biographer Susan Dworkin wrote in *Miss America, 1945:*

Bess Myerson and the Year That Changed Our Lives: "In the Jewish community she was the most famous pretty girl since Queen Esther." Myerson showed the world that beauty and brains *do* go together—and with great success. But something must have snapped. Sukhreet Gabel reported that Myerson came to her house during the trial and told her, "You keep your mouth shut." And while she awaited trial, the former Miss America was arrested for shoplifting $44.07 worth of cosmetics and flashlights in a drugstore. Her net worth at the time was estimated to be $16 million.

Bess Myerson eventually moved to California, and led a quiet, reclusive life. When she died there at the age of 90 in 2014, she was still the only Jewish Miss America ever crowned.

DANIEL ROSTENKOWSKI

(1928–2010)

O f *course* it was too good to be true. That's why they call it "illegal."

One of the oddest scams ever to hit Washington had to be the House Post Office Scandal in the early 1990s. It had all the earmarks of a great crime movie: money laundering, corrupt congressmen, and a crazy scheme involving postage stamps. By the end of the brouhaha, it put more than one politician—and a postmaster—out of business.

At the center of the controversy was Representative Daniel Rostenkowski, a Chicago politician of the old order, son of an alderman and influential committeeman of the mostly Polish 32nd Ward. He had been a four-letter varsity athlete in high school, went on to do a stint in the United States Army, and was elected as a Democrat to the Illinois House of Representatives in 1952 at the age of twenty-four, while he was still finishing his belated post-Army college education.

Rostenkowski was an ally of Chicago's long-running Richard J. Daley political machine, and though he moved to Washington in 1959 when he entered Congress, "Rosty" was a Windy City guy through and through, commuting back to his hometown nearly every weekend. His career in D.C. had its ups and downs, but in 1981 he finally hit it big and became chairman of the powerful House Ways and Means Committee. There he was known, as the *Los Angeles Times* put it, as "an unparalleled master of arm-twisting and deal-cutting." He is, however, perhaps best known for becoming embroiled in a scandal that became known in the press as the House Post Office Scandal.

It all started with a whisper and a single person under suspicion, as so many blowups do. By 1992, it worked its way up to House Postmaster Robert V. Rota, which is when the fireworks began. Dan Rostenkowski and Rep. Joe Kolter of Pennsylvania were named by the Postmaster and became the heart of the investigation. The investigation was related to a scheme involving postage stamps. Or to be more clear, a lack of stamps.

The scam was simple, but it was sweet. Congress members and their staff are given postal privileges to send official mail at no cost; people had taken advantage of it for years, sending personal mail, Christmas cards, and the like. But eventually it became clear that more than the occasional birthday card was slipping through. Lawmakers had figured out an easy way to embezzle government money. They would use congressional funds, vouchers, or campaign checks to purchase stamps at the House Post Office, but then one of two things would happen: either they were given cash instead of stamps, or else they purchased the stamps and returned them in exchange for cash several days later. Either way, it was money laundering, plain and simple. There were also charges against both Rostenkowski and Kolter regarding misuse of government funds at the House Stationery store. (Kolter's shopping sprees in particular were fairly extensive. In 1994, the *Los Angeles Times* reported that he was indicted for buying more than $33,000 worth of merchandise between 1986 and 1991, including "650 pieces of china and glassware, 40 watches and clocks, 30 Mont Blanc pens, 30 pieces of luggage and 2 gold necklaces.")

Rostenkowski was eventually indicted for other breaches as well: jury tampering and hiring "ghost" employees for no-show jobs. In the end, he pleaded guilty to two charges of mail fraud and was sentenced to seventeen months in prison and a $100,000 fine. The case was handled by Eric Holder, who would go on to be the future United States attorney general.

The shock waves that the House Post Office Scandal generated turned out to be less about the stealing and more about the downfall of the Dan Rostenkowski. His indictment and conviction signaled an end to the era of old-school politics. "Rosty" was a rare-steak-and-whiskey kind of guy, used to deal-making politics and big city political machines. He did favors and asked for them in return—and he was used to that being the way things got done. No one was more shocked than he was that this was no longer the case. He insisted, even after he pleaded guilty, that he had merely violated House rules, not broken the law. He just didn't get it—this was the way things had always been done!

Former president Gerald Ford wrote only one pardon letter after he left the White House, and it was on Rostenkowski's behalf. In his letter, Ford wrote, "Danny's problem was he played precisely under the rules of the city of Chicago. Now, those aren't the same rules that any other place in the country lives by, but in Chicago they were *totally* legal, and Danny got a screwing." Well, perhaps what Rostenkowski did was not totally legal, but it certainly was commonplace. A more balanced view came from David E. Rosenbaum in the *New York Times*:

> He is a throwback to an earlier era—to a time when Congress was dominated by a few giants, when big-city political machines were central influences in the Democratic Party, when personal loyalty was valued more in politics than ideology and when passing laws was more important than public relations. . . . Mr. Rostenkowski's perception of what is expected of a Congressman has not kept up with the times.

President Clinton pardoned Dan Rostenkowski in 2001. By that time, he had set up a consulting firm back in Chicago and was collecting a hefty federal pension that exceeded $125,000 yearly. (Pensions are based on length of service, and Rostenkowski had served thirty-six years in Congress.) The Post Office Scandal was part of what put the Republicans back in the majority in the House back in 1994. A group of young freshmen congressmen elected in 1990—called the "Gang of Seven"—led the charge in cleaning up congressional leadership. Two of these newbies made their chops back then, and it doesn't seem to have hurt John Boehner and Rick Santorum's careers at all.

MEL REYNOLDS

(1952–)

Americans are fully aware that there are perks when you're a politician. Maybe there's a limo here or some fancy meals there. But Mel Reynolds seemed to think he was entitled to much, much more.

Melvin Reynolds was a Democratic rising star, and his run for Congress from the state of Illinois in 1992 looked like it was going to be just the beginning of an auspicious career. One half of a pair of twin sons of a Mississippi preacher who had moved north to Chicago as a child, Mel spun his associates degree into a masters in Public Administration from Harvard and then a Rhodes Scholarship at Oxford, where he earned his law degree. For several years, he relied on that education as an associate professor of political science. But in the late

1980s, Reynolds decided he'd like to enter the political arena. He twice lost a run for Congress. In 1992, the third time was the charm.

It didn't take long for that long-desired political career to start crumbling. Before his first two-year term was over, Mel Reynolds had been indicted for sexual assault and abuse with sixteen-year-old campaign volunteer Beverly Heard. However, with no opposition for his seat and his continued denial of any wrongdoing, he was sworn in for a second term in Washington. By the time Reynolds finally went to court for the sexual assault accusation in 1995, the story was suddenly extremely muddy: in January, Heard recanted her story and then cooled her heels in jail for two weeks when she refused to testify against Reynolds. By August, she'd changed her tune. "It was a consensual sexual relationship," Heard testified in court, "but I don't think he deserves to go to jail." But the age of sexual consent in Illinois was eighteen, whether Heard gave consent or not.

Heard eventually revealed that she and Reynolds had been having sex—on the phone or in person—two or three times a week during the 1992 campaign. And Reynolds's sexual exploits with Heard were only a part of what investigations uncovered. There were several counts of child pornography against him as well. Reynolds was convicted on August 22, 1995 on twelve counts of sexual assault, obstruction of justice, and solicitation of child pornography. He was sentenced to five years in jail, and on October 1 of that year, he resigned his House seat.

In 1996, just a year after the former congressman put on his orange jumpsuit, Reynolds and his wife Marisol faced a new list of charges, including wire fraud, bank fraud, making false statement on loan applications, conspiracy to defraud the Federal Election Commission, and making false statements to the election committee. On top of that, Mel Reynolds was charged with defrauding several banks, using false statement to procure personal loans. The sixteen new charges he was convicted of added seventy-eight more months onto his prison sentence, but he was released in 2001 by a commutation from outgoing president Bill Clinton. He had no home to go to, as Marisol had turned on him in 1996 and reported that he abused her and forced her help with defrauding the government. She had moved out with their three children. Instead, Jesse Jackson took him in and gave Reynolds a job at his Rainbow/PUSH Coalition.

A more humble man may have assumed his political chances were in the past, but not Mel Reynolds. He wanted to take back his congressional seat, and so he ran in 2004 against Jesse Jackson Jr., the son of the man who had so graciously supported him when he was down and out. Jackson Jr. won by a landslide, bringing in 88% of the primary votes. When Jackson retired in 2012 from his seat, Reynolds tried again, but suffered another unsuccessful run.

And then Mel Reynolds went global. In 2014, he was arrested in Zimbabwe. Not only had the former congressman overstayed his visa, but he had apparently also overstayed his welcome at a hotel where he now owed well over $20,000. Due to the immigration violation on the visa, he was deported to South Africa. When last heard from in March 2014, Reynolds told the Associated Press that he was being pursued by a secret Zimbabwean death squad for knowledge he has of illegal American business in that country.

As for Beverly Heard, she went into the air force, announced she was a lesbian, and has written several books; she now goes by the name Solomohn Ennis. In 2008, upon the publication of her book, she told a local Chicago news channel, "I've been to college, I've worked. But what is of most important is how I've pulled together what has happened to me."

ROD BLAGOJEVICH

(1956–)

R od Blagojevich was the kind of guy who believed everything had a price. And he thought he had the Golden Goose to sell. Knowing that Senator Barack Obama's Illinois Senate seat would be vacant in January 2009 when he assumed the presidency, and knowing that, by law, the Illinois governor appoints the successor, Governor Blagojevich believed he had a golden opportunity.

On a recorded phone call, Blagojevich was heard talking about Obama's seat. "I've got this thing, and it's fucking golden," he said on the recording. "I'm just not giving it up for fucking nothing." Later in the call, he went on to say, "If I don't get what I want . . . I'll just take the Senate seat myself." But Blagojevich wouldn't get the Senate seat or that cash payoff. He'd get a prison sentence instead.

Rob Blagojevich was born and raised in Chicago, the son of Serbian immigrants who had moved to the United States several years before his birth. He worked hard as a kid, shining shoes, delivering pizza, washing dishes. In his late teens, he became a successful amateur boxer for a short time, until he lost by a TKO in only the third round of a Golden Gloves competition. He called it quits and never fought again. So it wouldn't be athletic fame for Blagojevich. Instead, he took an alternate route to the American Dream: college, law school, and politics.

Blagojevich worked in the state attorney's office until he saw an opening for a state House seat and went for it in 1992 with the help of his powerful father-in-law, Chicago alderman Richard Mell. In 1996, he finally made it to Washington as a Democratic United States congressman, and ultimately to the governor's office after the 2002 election. His career so far was not studded with accolades, but in the next few years, Blagojevich would make plenty of headlines.

In his move to the governor's mansion, Blagojevich joined an infamous club. Six previous Illinois governors had been indicted or arrested—three since 1971. Blagojevich was about to be the next.

Though he managed to get reelected in 2006, and he worked hard on issues such as health care and gun control, Blagojevich made several missteps. First, he commissioned expensive highway signage with his name on it, which would have to be replaced when he left. Then he got a "deal" on foreign flu vaccines to the tune of $2.6 million; all of it had to be dumped when the FDA refused to allow the medication into the country. Two of his senior staff members were indicted on charges of kickbacks. It was also reported that he'd accepted a $1,500 check from a state worker which was purportedly a gift for one of his children . . . but he couldn't remember which child and for what occasion.

What finally brought impeachment hearings down on Rod Blagojevich's head was the aforementioned vacant Obama Senate seat. The governor had big plans and even bigger payoffs in mind for himself. It was all "pay to play," and if you didn't have campaign contributions, favors, special access, or just plain old money to offer, you were never going to get on Blagojevich's short list for the Senate job.

The feds caught wind of the scheme to sell Senator Obama's former position to the highest bidder, and U.S. Attorney Patrick Fitzgerald got permission for a wiretap, which clinched the evidence they needed for an arrest.

On December 9, 2008, the FBI arrested the governor on several corruption charges, including his illegal plans for the replacement of the Senate seat. Then, on January 8, 2009, the Illinois house voted to impeach Rod Blagojevich—in a vote of 114–1. By the time Blagojevich was convicted on seventeen counts in 2011, fifteen members of his staff had been indicted. At that point, the former governor had already been out of a job for two years, except for a brief foray working for Donald Trump on *The Celebrity Apprentice.* Goodbye, American dream.

Even after the Selling of the Senate Seat debacle, Blagojevich somehow managed to make things worse. In a 2010 interview with *Esquire* magazine, he said, "I'm blacker than

Barack Obama. I shined shoes. I grew up in a five-room apartment. My father had a little laundromat in a black community not far from where we lived. I saw it all growing up." Blago had become more than a liability to Illinois; he had become a national laughingstock, with late-night jokes made about both his hubris and that hairdo. (Oh, the hairdo.)

Several months after his arrest, Blagojevich said, "I don't believe there's any cloud that hangs over me. I think there's nothing but sunshine hanging over me." The current date for Blago to see any sunshine—outside of the prison yard, at least—is May 23, 2024.

MICHAEL GRIMM

(1970–)

C ongressman Michael Grimm's path seemed a promising one from the start. A boy from Queens, New York, he graduated from his local Catholic high school and went into the marines. After his stint in the service, he returned home for college, graduated magna cum laude from New York Law School in 2002, and started a career with the FBI. During his time there, he spent two years undercover as a stockbroker for a Wall Street sting. Upon leaving the FBI, Grimm went into the growing health food business, buying a restaurant in Manhattan. And then in 2010, the former marine successfully ran for Congress in New York's Staten Island, with endorsements from some of the top GOP politicians in the country, including Rudy Giuliani, Sarah Palin, John McCain, and George H. W. Bush.

But things are often not what they seem. From felony tax evasion to perjury to extremely fishy campaign contributions from his 2010 congressional run and trouble from dealings with his Healthalicious restaurant, Grimm managed to rack up a twenty-count federal indictment. He pleaded guilty to just two. In 2014, despite his initial blustery insistence that he would not step down from his congressional, he resigned.

Grimm's fall from grace made national headlines in part due to an on-screen moment he shared with a political journalist following the national State of the Union address in January 2014. The exchange took place just minutes after President Barack Obama's speech, when Michael Scotto, a newsman working for a New York City–based news channel, met with Representative Grimm for a promised one-on-one. Standing against the backdrop of the Capitol building's upper rotunda, all marble and grandeur, Scotto began to ask Grimm questions about the ongoing FBI investigation against him. As far as the congressman was concerned, this was not part of the interview deal. He refused to answer and stormed off, only to return once again after a surprised Scotto had signed off. In his rage, Michael Grimm forgot the number one rule in the life of a politician: the camera is always on. The still-rolling camera caught the following exchange:

> GRIMM: Let me be clear to you. If you ever do that to me again I'll throw you off this fucking balcony.
> SCOTTO: Why, why, I just wanted to ask you . . .
> GRIMM: If you ever do that to me again . . .
> SCOTTO: Why? Why? It's a valid question.

GRIMM: You're not man enough. I'll break you in
half. Like a boy.

Of course Scotto didn't bring down Michael Grimm.
Grimm did that all by himself. But he did start off the congressman's annus horribilis with a jaw-dropping bang. It was
enough to keep the ex-congressman out of the eye of the
camera for a good long while.

NO GUTS, NO GLORY

You have to be a certain type of person to get to the top of the political heap. And when you're talking about the Oval Office, it's an incredible, dog-eat–dog climb to get there, followed by the tightrope act that is the American presidency. As a result, bad colds, crybabies, and broken hearts simply aren't allowed—because it doesn't get tougher than this.

WILLIAM HENRY HARRISON

(1773–1841)

Thirty days, twelve hours, and thirty minutes. That's how long William Henry Harrison held office as ninth president of the United States. He had been a war hero, having gained notoriety at the Battle of Tippecanoe by holding back Tecumseh and the Shawnee. With seasoned politician John Tyler by his side as a vice presidential candidate, they defeated incumbent Martin Van Buren and popularized the use of a campaign song called "Tip and Ty" that would become perhaps the best-remembered part of the entire campaign:

What's the cause of this commotion, motion, motion,
Our country through?
It is the ball a-rolling on

For Tippecanoe and Tyler too.
For Tippecanoe and Tyler too.
And with them we'll beat little Van, Van, Van,
Van is a used up man.
And with them we'll beat little Van.

It was off to Washington for Harrison and Tyler. The new president worked hard at his inauguration speech, and even though he got his friend and famed orator Daniel Webster to come in and edit it, the address was still 8,445 words long and took nearly two entire cold, wet, bone-chilling hours to get through. How he chose to appear at the speech may have sealed his fate.

Harrison was a farmer, so he was used to braving inclement weather. Perhaps he wanted to make his first presidential appearance look strong, because he decided on that cold, rainy March day to deliver his never-ending speech without a coat, hat, or gloves. The inaugural address was followed by a full day of hoopla and then three inaugural balls, by which time Harrison had developed the chills. The chills turned into a cold, and then pleurisy and pneumonia. To be fair, this all took about three weeks, so whether or not you believe it could be traced back to inauguration day depends what you think about old wives' tales. Nevertheless, that's how the doctors treated it: as a result of cold caught at the inauguration. And treat him they did. They tried every trick they knew: leeches, castor oil, opium, even something to do with live snakes. But on April 4, the 68-year-old new president succumbed. The cause of death was listed as "pneumonia of the lower lobe of the right lung."

For more than two centuries, the bad weather–inauguration story held fast, until 2014, when a *New York Times* story reported that the probable cause of the death of President Harrison was enteric, or typhoid, fever. Where he contracted it is even more horrifying. Apparently sewage and "night soil," or human excrement, stagnated in a marsh only a few blocks from the White House. It is very possible that the marsh was infecting the drinking water in the White House. It may be no coincidence that two other presidents from the 1840s— Zachary Taylor and James K. Polk—suffered from severe gastrointestinal problems.

As for the fetid, toxic, poisonous, Washington swamp? Insert your own joke here.

JAMES BUCHANAN
(1791–1868)

Worst president ever.

Franklin Pierce and poor William Henry Harrison, with his one-month term, are often mentioned as possible titleholders for the least effective president in American history. But James Buchanan always seems to come out on top—or bottom, depending on how you look at it. Why so?

James Buchanan started out as a bit of a dark horse. His predecessor Franklin Pierce was absolutely certain he would be elected for a second term. Pierce had appointed Buchanan as ambassador to the Court of St. James, and so Buchanan was still hanging around London until March of the 1856 election year. Buchanan never even declared himself a candidate for the Democratic Party. In fact, he had told Nathaniel Hawthorne only the year before that, following his London stint, he was coming home to retire. At sixty-five, he was too old to think about leading the country, he said. Yet Buchanan ended up getting the nomination and accepting it. (Those were the days: no caucusing, no collecting skeletons from the closet, no newly published autobiographies. Candidates just sashayed into the fray a few months beforehand.) In his inaugural speech on March 4, 1857, Buchanan announced that he would not seek a second term. Way to wow your crowd.

By the time Buchanan took office, the most volatile issue in the country was slavery, and Americans hoped the new president could calm the increasingly roiling waters between North and South. But Buchanan was conflicted; he was morally opposed to slavery himself, but he felt that the Constitution protected it. The citizens knew it. Southerners were generally suspicious of this North/South-straddling Pennsylvanian, while people in the North called him a "dough face," a northerner with southern sympathies. Buchanan hid behind the law again when talk of secession started, stating that not only was secession illegal but so was going to war over it. When the Civil War started just months after he left office, Buchanan supported it, but there was a huge amount of public blowback blaming him for the war, and few came to his defense. He was roundly criticized for having failed to take a stance in either direction.

But Buchanan's political ineptitude isn't the only thing for which he is remembered. Throughout his life, he was plagued by speculation about his sexuality. To this day, Buchanan remains the only bachelor commander-in-chief. Buchanan been engaged early on, in 1818, to Ann Coleman, but she died before their wedding day. There were some who said Buchanan was only marrying her for her fortune, that she knew it, and purposely overdosed on laudanum. Her father did not even let Buchanan attend the funeral.

Buchanan never had a romance with a woman after that. He did, however, spend a decade of his life—from 1834 to 1844—living with William Rufus DeVane King, then an Alabama senator. Their relationship seemed rather an open secret in Washington; in various social circles, they were referred to as "the Siamese Twins" (common slang at the time for a gay couple) or "Miss Nancy" and "Aunt Fancy." The cozy arrangement was only interrupted when King became minister of France in 1844 and moved to Europe. Following his duties in France, Rufus DeVane King would go on to become America's only bachelor vice president, serving under Franklin Pierce. King died in 1853, before Buchanan became chief executive, and though Buchanan ordered his correspondence burned upon his death (a strange directive in itself), a letter that he wrote to his friend Cornelia Roosevelt after King's departure to France seems to confirm their relationship:

> I am now "solitary and alone," having no companion in the house with me. I have gone a-wooing to several gentlemen, but have not succeeded with any one of them. I feel that it is not good for a man to be alone; and should not be astonished to find myself married to some old maid who can nurse me when I am sick, provide good dinners for me when I am well, and not expect from me any very ardent or romantic affection.

Sounds like a real catch.

When President Buchanan's four years were done, he could not wait to hightail it out of office and was thrilled to keep his promise from his inaugural speech to depart the White House. In fact, as he accompanied his successor Abraham Lincoln to the new president's inauguration, Buchanan said, "If you are as happy entering the presidency as I am leaving it, then you are a very happy man."

With the intense and widespread blame for the Civil War that followed him in retirement, plus what sounds like a fairly lonely existence, James Buchanan's last years were not spent basking in the afterglow of a presidential job well done. The day before he died at seventy-seven, he said optimistically, "History will vindicate my memory."

Not likely, Mr. President.

EDWARD MUSKIE

(1914–1996)

Two things are particularly memorable about the presidential election of 1972: first, it was the first in which the voting age was dropped from twenty-one to eighteen, and second, most of those young voters were behind Richard Nixon's Democratic opponent, George McGovern, the liberal anti–Vietnam War contender. McGovern lost, of course, carrying only the state of Massachusetts, but still, he had a pretty good run. The thing is, it's very possible he may not have even gotten the party bid at all if Maine senator Edmund Muskie hadn't broken down and cried on the steps of the *Manchester Union-Leader* newspaper offices while campaigning in New Hampshire.

Many thought Muskie was the only man capable of defeating Nixon, and they may have been right. Evidently Nixon's "dirty tricks" gang thought so. The president's camp had Muskie in their sights, and Nixon's deputy director of communications Kenneth W. Clawson took his job a step too far. He wrote and anonymously mailed a letter to the *Union-Leader* that would become known as the "Canuck letter."

The letter was received at the newspaper just two weeks before the New Hampshire primary, and the *Union-Leader's* decision to publish it surprised no one, as publisher William Loeb was a staunch Nixon supporter. Fraught with bad spelling and terrible handwriting, the letter had purportedly been written by someone who had had a previous conversation with Muskie in which the senator had glibly used the term "Canuck," a derogatory word for French Canadians. The letter seemed questionable from the start. Muskie was a Maine man born and bred, having served as governor and then a United States senator for more than a decade. It would be unlikely that he would feel that way about a group who make up a good part of New England's constituency, and it would be sheer political suicide for him to voice his feelings even if he did. While that pot was stewing, Loeb completed his one-two punch a couple of days later when the *Union-Leader* reprinted a story from *Newsweek* which said Muskie's wife Jane was known to have a couple of drinks on the campaign trail and told dirty jokes with the press corps. This was the straw that broke the candidate's back.

Just a few days before the primary, Muskie held a press conference on the steps of the newspaper's office, fervently defending his wife and railing against Loeb and his reporting practices. "This man doesn't walk, he crawls," Muskie said, and then, in front of God and everyone, began to cry. The candidate later insisted that it was snowflakes, not tears, that everyone saw on TV. This was unlikely, but no matter, as the damage was done. Though Muskie still won the primary, many New Hampshire Democrats fled to McGovern's camp. Muskie's fan base nationwide began to falter, as nobody wanted a crybaby president, and so McGovern got the nomination. Ken Clawson bragged to friends about forging the Canuck letter himself, (and further down the line, the Watergate investigation would prove that). And so, at least for the 1972 White House election, Nixon and his band of dirty tricksters had won.

CRAZY IN
THE CAPITOL

Voters send them to Washington, put them all together, and expected them to play together nicely. Fat chance. Some legislators think life under the rotunda is just a big playground; others are just lucky to get out alive.

SAMUEL J. TILDEN

(1814–1886)

n the world of you-wuz-robbed presidential politics, the
Al Gore–George W. Bush dustup first comes to mind. But
their vote-counting battle was not the first. That record
is held by Rutherford B. Hayes and Samuel J. Tilden in the
presidential election of 1876.

Both men had reputable careers as politicians. Hayes was a
one-term Republican congressman from Ohio who had served
two terms as governor; Tilden had served as a Democratic New
York State assemblyman and also as governor of the Empire
State. Like another famous New York politician—Michael
Bloomberg—Tilden had made a reputation for himself as a
smart, wealthy businessman. It seemed like a fair match for

ERIN McHUGH

the title of commander-in-chief, but that may have been the last fair thing about it.

When Election Day came and the votes were counted, Tilden won handily in the popular vote, ahead by some 250,000. But the winner would also need 185 electoral votes. Tilden had 184 to Hayes's 165, and there were 20 votes still in contention, as Florida, Louisiana, and South Carolina had each submitted two sets of electoral votes to Congress. Fraud was suspected on both sides. A congressional committee comprised of three Democrats, three Republicans, and an independent seemed to be the logical answer to settle the issue. But when the independent member dropped out and a fourth Republican was added to the mix, Tilden seemed to be sunk.

This is where all the tricky stuff began. An unwritten, undocumented agreement, now known as the Compromise of 1877, took shape and, as with all compromises, each party got something and nobody left completely happy. All the electoral votes went to Rutherford B. Hayes, with several promises on his part for clinching this deal, most importantly, that all federal troops had to leave the former Confederate states. This put a Republican in the White House, but ostensibly ended Reconstruction in the South, turning it over to the Democrats.

Tilden had been silent during the several months all this waiting and confabbing went on, and many of his devotees were miffed; they had wanted him to fight the good fight for what they believed was his right to the Oval Office. But upon the announcement of his loss, he said, "I can retire to public life with the consciousness that I shall receive from posterity the credit of having been elected to the highest position in the gift of the people, without any of the cares and responsibilities of the office."

However, Tilden had not skulked off as quietly as folks thought. He still had a fan base, and there was talk of him garnering the Democratic nomination for the 1880 election; Hayes had promised that he would serve only one term, so that problem was already out of the way. Then, in 1878, the *New York Tribune* reported that perhaps Tilden hadn't taken the presidential election melee lying down after all. There was evidence that Team Tilden had offered bribes to buy the electoral votes in the three contested states. Samuel Tilden claimed innocence and volunteered to appear before a Congressional subcommittee, which indeed found him innocent of all claims. But perception being everything in politics, the race was lost before it started. Samuel Tilden bowed out of politics for good.

Rutherford B. Hayes would always be half-jokingly called "His Fraudulency" by historians. Meanwhile, Samuel J. Tilden went on to donate many of his millions to build a library in New York City and has a plethora of streets, towns, a ship, and perhaps even a cocktail named after him. His grave carries the legend "I Still Trust in the People."

PRESTON BROOKS

(1819–1857)

I t was North vs. South at its worst.

Though the Civil War will always be the final say on the matter of slavery, the actions of Congressman Preston Brooks in the Senate chamber on May 22, 1856, could hardly be a more vivid representation of how divided the country had become.

At the center of what transpired on that day was the question of Kansas, that rectangle smack in the middle of the United States whose future as a free or slave state was bringing abolitionists and pro-slavery factions to a boil. The Kansas-Nebraska Act of 1854 had opened up Kansas to the possibility of becoming a slave state, negating the Missouri Compromise of 1820, which had left Kansas as a territory free of slavery. It was now left up to the residents of Kansas to make this momentous decision, and Northerners were certain that wealthy slave owners would move in and change the state's status.

The vicious attack in which Brooks was involved took place two years after the Kansas-Nebraska Act was passed, demonstrating how fervent the feelings were on both sides of the issue. On May 20, Senator Charles Sumner of Massachusetts gave a speech called "The Crime Against Kansas," proposing that Kansas immediately be admitted to the Union as a free state. He called it "the rape of a virgin territory"— pretty strong language for the mid–nineteenth century—and decried the authors of the Kansas-Nebraska Act, Stephen A. Douglas of Illinois (and Lincoln-debating fame) and Andrew Butler of South Carolina. It was Butler's kin who took offense and made it his business to defend the family honor.

Two days after Sumner's speech, Preston Brooks—Butler's cousin and a pro-slavery champion of the South—stormed into the Senate chamber to find Sumner sitting at his desk, catching up on correspondence. His first attack was verbal: "Mr. Sumner, I have read your speech twice over carefully. It is a libel on South Carolina, and Mr. Butler, who is a relative of mine." His second attack was physical; he began to beat Senator Sumner with his gold-headed cane. (Brooks had to walk with a cane because he had been injured in a duel over a political difference of opinion some years before; this was not his first go-round.) Since the desks in the chamber were bolted to the floor, Sumner—who had been taken by surprise—tried to escape, but got stuck trying to free himself. Brooks continued to beat him until Sumner could not see through his own blood; he finally tore the desk from the floor and tried to escape, only to collapse in the aisle of the chamber. Those who tried to help him were blocked by another Southern congressman, a friend of Brooks's, who brandished a gun to hold them at bay.

While Northerners and abolitionists vilified Brooks's attack, the pro-slavery camp hailed him as a hero. He received hundreds of canes to replace the one he had broken in half while beating up Sumner. (One cane was even inscribed with HIT HIM AGAIN.) Those on both sides of the aisle thought Sumner's speech was excessive in its use of harsh and racy language, but Brooks had to be held accountable for his actions. He was charged with assault in a District of Columbia court and fined $300, but received no prison sentence. In the ensuing furor, Brooks resigned in order to let his constituency decide on his fate; to no one's surprise, they overwhelmingly voted him back in.

As for Charles Sumner, his extensive injuries, which today we would call traumatic brain injury and post-traumatic stress disorder, kept him from returning to the Senate for three years. In solidarity, the voters of Massachusetts reelected him in the interim and kept his seat absent until his return. And in perhaps a karmic stroke, Preston Brooks died less than a year after his attack on Charles Sumner.

One enormously positive effect of the attack on Sumner was that it strengthened the nascent anti-slavery Republican Party—the party that would soon bring Abraham Lincoln to the White House.

THOMAS LINDSAY BLANTON

(1872–1957)

The utter shame Thomas Lindsay Blanton brought to the floor of the House of Representatives in 1921 was the result of a letter—and not even a letter he had written himself. Laughingly tame by today's standards, it was front-page news back in the day. But it nearly caused his expulsion from Congress.

Blanton was a staunchly anti-union Democrat from Texas, vehement about voicing his position at every opportunity. He decided to demonstrate the rancor between union and non-union groups to his congressional brethren by reading a letter sent by non-union government printer Millard French to Levi Huber, a union printer. Blanton wanted to show how unsavory the relationship between the two camps was by having the letter printed in the daily Congressional Record. He made sure to bring it to the government printing office on a Saturday in order to fly under the radar. The language in the letter was considered so horrendous that one member of the House said, "Any one speaking the words contained in the Congressional Record would be subject to fine and imprisonment under the laws of the land." Herewith the scalding words in question, in their original form:

> G__d D___n your black heart, you ought to have it torn out of you, you u____ s_____ of a b_____. You and the Public Printer has no sense. You k_____ his a____ and he is a d_____d fool for letting you do it.

Congress was livid that language like this was slipped into the Record. A resolution for Thomas Blanton's expulsion from Congress resulted in a vote of 203 to 113, not the two-thirds majority to carry. But a second vote to censure him was 293 to 0. Representative Franklin Mondell, who led the charge to oust Blanton, said, "There is not a member who will not say that it is the vilest thing he has ever seen in print." Meanwhile Blanton insisted, "Any woman or child could read all that I have printed without a single blush of shame." The act was pure trickery on Representative Blanton's part, it's true, and he certainly had his own agenda. But perhaps the most interesting part was that the punishment that rained down upon him was for an incident that didn't even involve his own words.

The censure shocked Thomas Blanton. He responded, "I have been here to prevent this Government from becoming Sovietized. I have spent piece after piece of property. I have caused first one good, fine bungalow to be gotten ready for sale, and then another, and my good wife consented each time. When you kick me out today, I shall go home with borrowed money to pay my railroad fare."

He did not get "kicked out," but following the announcement of his censure, he left the chamber, fell in a faint in the corridor, hit his head on the marble floor, and retired to his office in tears.

But one shouldn't think Blanton soft on practically anything. During his time in Congress, he favored a "work or fight" amendment to the draft law during World War I; he stood against the railroad strike of 1921, despite being threatened several times and having someone shoot at his car; and he backed unpopular proposals to stop immigration for five years (1924), then again for seven years (1928). In 1935, he introduced a bill to outlaw Communists. Overall, he was so thumbs-down on any proposed congressional junkets and fringe benefits that he managed to irk colleagues on both sides of the aisle.

Perhaps surprisingly, after Thomas Blanton's throwdown in Congress in 1921, he managed to recover. Once he got back up from that stony corridor floor, he got reelected by Texas voters. Perhaps they simply admired his spunk.

ADAM CLAYTON POWELL JR.

(1908–1972)

Adam Clayton Powell Jr. was a textbook example of a hero of the people—or maybe a movie version, what with his handsome, debonair looks. He was the son of a powerful Harlem preacher, Adam Clayton Powell Sr., who had been born into poverty and educated at Yale before becoming an early civil rights leader with charisma to spare. With parents who were both of mixed race, Powell, Jr. was light-skinned, and by the time he arrived at Colgate University, he began to pass as white. It was more of a sin of omission than an outright lie; he just never mentioned he was black. One famous story features Powell traveling on a train as a young man, and when someone shouted, "There's a nigger on this train!" Powell calmly asked, "Where?"

Powell earned a master's degree in religious education and became a prominent community activist in Harlem, where his father was the pastor of the famed Abyssinian Baptist Church. Months after his graduation from Colgate, he began service as an assistant pastor at Abyssinian and director of Abyssinian's Kitchen and Relief operations, a service which was integral to Harlem residents during the Great Depression. He was following in his esteemed father's footsteps.

Powell worked with the people of Harlem outside the environs of the church, too—organizing protests and attempting to bring local jobs and affordable housing to the black community. He even led a "Shop Only Where You Can Work" crusade on 125th Street, causing shutdowns and an ensuing change of hiring policies in many stores. His efforts brought more people into the church, and Powell then made his mark outside his neighborhood when he picketed for more black jobs with the Metropolitan Transit Authority and at the 1939 World's Fair in Queens. In 1938, he took over as pastor at Abyssinian Baptist Church.

By that point, Adam Clayton Powell Jr. had political ambitions, and in 1941 he won a place on the powerful New York City Council—the first African American to do so. He would also be the first black congressman from New York when he went to Washington representing Harlem in 1945. Around this time, he divorced his first wife, Isabel Washington, and married his second, Hazel Scott, with whom he had a son, Adam Clayton Powell III. Adam Clayton Powell IV would be born during his father's third marriage, to Yvette Flores Diago, and would go on to serve as a New York City councilman.

Civil rights were the main thrust of Powell's congressional campaign, and once in office, he challenged racist protocols regularly, such as ignoring WHITES ONLY signs in bathrooms and other facilities on Capitol Hill and bringing black patrons to the all-white House dining room. Most importantly, Powell broke the unspoken rule that new congressmen do not speak on the floor during their first year. When John Rankin of Mississippi used the word "nigger" on the House floor, Powell stood and asked for his impeachment. Adam Clayton Powell Jr. remained in Congress and fought the good fight, finally attaining a chairmanship in 1961 on the House Education and Labor Committee. Powell's work there would be prodigious, and President Johnson would later commend him for passing "forty-nine pieces of bedrock legislation" after five years as chairman.

But it was also at this point that the tide began to turn on the reputation of the activist congressman. In 1958, he was indicted for income tax evasion, and though he narrowly escaped conviction by a hung jury, the government continued looking into his finances. Trouble came again in 1960, when he accused Harlem widow Esther James on television of being a "bag woman" and collecting money for corrupt police. She sued him for libel and was awarded $211,500. Powell refused to pay and stopped visiting his district at all except for Sundays, knowing he wouldn't be served papers by court officials on the week's holiest day.

From there, things fell apart rather quickly for Powell. Investigations stepped up on his finances, particularly regarding his use of government funds for travel, mostly to his home in Bimini. He felt, evidently, that misuse of the people's money was commonplace and expected. "I will always do just what every other congressman and committee chairman has done and is doing and will do." (Powell later alleged that the head of the investigating committee himself "took a House dining-room waiter on a junket to Paris.") In 1967, Powell was stripped of his committee chairmanship. That same year, Yvette Diago—the third Mrs. Powell—admitted that she had been listed as a no-show on her husband's payroll for years; in fact, it seemed she was still listed on the books, even though they were by then divorced.

There were many in Congress who believed losing the chairmanship was not a stiff enough punishment for Powell. In a vote, he was ousted from Congress altogether. Back in Harlem, however, Adam Clayton Powell Jr. remained the preacher hero. He ran for his own congressional seat, to fill his own vacancy, and won it by nearly an 80% majority. He paid Congress a fine, was told by the Supreme Court that his removal had been unconstitutional, and stayed in that congressional seat from Harlem until 1971. It seems Adam Clayton Powell Jr. took his own advice—the same advice he famously gave to his constituents over the years: "Keep the faith, baby."

INDICTED, CENSURED & IMPEACHED

Scrolling through the annals of American history, it becomes clear how often the people we've entrusted are brought before their brethren with the possibility of punishment at stake. Many times—too many to count—a slap on the wrist is all that happens. But every once in a while, badly behaving politicians get exactly what they deserve.

MATTHEW LYON

(1749–1822)

Matthew Lyon was born in Ireland and came to the United States in 1765 as was what was called a redemptioner, an immigrant who was basically an indentured servant until he paid back his passage. After a stint in Connecticut working on a farm, he moved to Vermont in 1774. He was a signer of the Declaration of Independence and joined the Continental Army—what a grand immigrant story!—and then the problems began.

First it was just a bump in the road: Lyon was temporarily but dishonorably discharged from the Continental Army in 1776. His company had revolted, and though he was later reinstated as a captain, that niggling discharge followed him throughout his life, easy fodder for any and all enemies to use. But he pulled it together after the discharge and went back home to help Vermont achieve statehood. He grew his manufacturing business there, founded a newspaper, and started running for political office. The fourth time was the charm for Matthew Lyon, and he was elected to the House of Representatives in 1797. Yet the very next year, Lyon earned the distinction of becoming the first member of Congress to be charged with an ethics violation for "gross indecency." These days, that brings to mind something along the lines of an Anthony Weiner–style debacle, but in yesteryear, it began with Lyon calling Congressman Roger Griswold a "scoundrel," which carried the weight of a four-letter insult in 1798. Lyon followed up by spitting tobacco juice in Griswold's eye. Evidently Griswold was the type to hold a grudge; a few weeks later, he attacked the "Spitting Lyon" on the floor of Congress and began beating him with a cane. Lyon managed to grab a pair of tongs to defend himself, and they were eventually pulled apart, none particularly the worse for wear. Since Lyon was the original instigator, the Ethics Committee recommended censure. The House, however, disagreed, and he stayed put with no punishment.

Before long, Matthew Lyon was at it again, but this time on a much grander scale. Lyon still owned his newspaper, and President John Adams had recently signed into law the Alien and Sedition Acts. Just as with the present-day Patriot Act, some people thought they were a boon to national security, while others believed the legislation was meant to suppress free speech—in this case, to silence those who were not Federalists like Adams. Or perhaps to muffle people like newspapermen. So when Lyon printed that President Adams had an "unbounded thirst for ridiculous pomp, foolish adulation, and selfish avarice," it wasn't long before he was carted off in shackles down the streets of Vergennes, Vermont, and thrown in jail. It was from that jail cell, incidentally, that he was reelected to Congress by a landslide—so add "only member of Congress to be reelected to his seat while in the pokey" to "first congressman to have an ethics charge filed against him."

Soon after that, in 1801, Matthew Lyon picked up and moved to the blue grasses of Kentucky, where he would go on to be a member of Congress for four terms.

ROBERT POTTER

(1800–1842)

R obert Potter was a seafaring lad from North Carolina, entering the United States Navy in 1815 when he was fifteen years old and staying in as a midshipman until he was twenty-one. In those days, life at sea provided plenty of excitement, from keeping on the lookout for pirates to policing the slave trade. He may have left the navy because he was discouraged at not being promoted, or, as legend has it, he may have gotten sacked because he killed an officer in a duel. Either way, it was back to the landlubber life and law school for Potter, who passed the bar in 1823. Potter then entered politics: first the North Carolina state legislature, and then Congress in 1829. His congressional career as a Tar Heel was even shorter than his time on the bounding main.

Because, on one summer afternoon in 1831, Robert Potter castrated two men.

Potter was certain that his wife, Isabella, was stepping out on him with two very different beaus—one a minister and the other a teenage boy. Some reports say that Mrs. Potter kept her affairs all in the family—that the minister was her cousin, and the boy was the nephew of her stepmother, but that's never been confirmed. What is known is that Potter attacked them both on the same day.

The particulars are sketchy, but reports of one assault say that when Potter found Isabella and the reverend in a buggy together, he roped the man of God around the neck, pulled him onto the ground, hogtied him, and then cut him down below.

As for the congressman, he was remorseful but seemingly at peace with his actions. He declared, "I am consoled by the conviction that in what I have done I have only acted upon those feelings which nature has implanted in the hearts of all men, indeed, I may say, of all animals; and that each of you would have done the same thing under the same circumstances." Well, maybe, maybe not. People may disagree with Potter's choice of punishment, but they certainly have not forgotten Congressman Potter's adventures with the knife. Even today, castration (or the threat of it, which is surely much more common) is still called "Potterizing" in parts of the South.

Following the incidents, Potter resigned from Congress in November of 1831, and he and his wife divorced. He paid a $3,000 fine and spent six months in prison. He did manage to get voted back into the legislature in 1834, but the next year got tossed out for an episode that involved a card game and such other shady dealings as cheating, brandishing a gun or a knife, stealing money, or trying to get out of a debt. (Take your pick; the reports vary.)

In 1835, Potter decided it was time to move to Texas. The Wild West seemed to better agree with the ruffian congressman. He got some military credibility back, and even ended up signing the Texas Declaration of Independence. He took up with a new woman, whom he "married" (though she seemed to still have a husband somewhere); he served as secretary of the navy (the Texan navy, that is) and even wormed his way back into (the Texan) Congress.

But perhaps Potter had not earned back quite enough karma points. In 1842, during a little-known Texan feud known as the Regulator–Moderator War, Potter found his home surrounded by members of the enemy Regulators. He thought he could get away by jumping into nearby Caddo Lake and escape by swimming underwater to safety. But the minute he came up for air, he was shot in the head. Robert Potter is buried in Texas and has a double-sided gravestone, with one side highlighting his political achievements in North Carolina, and the other side, Texas.

THE PHONE-JAMMING SCANDAL
(2002)

The casual political observer would say that United States senator Jeanne Shaheen's career has been extremely successful, and they would be right. But there was a hiccup in her career back in 2002, when, after three terms as New Hampshire's governor, Shaheen narrowly lost a bid for a United States Senate seat to Republican congressman John Sununu. When the two candidates paired up for the next senatorial contest in 2008, Shaheen came out the victor. In retrospect, Shaheen laid blame for the 2002 loss on her constituency's disenchantment with some of her gubernatorial decisions, but a phone-jamming scandal with national implications may have had much more to do with her not getting the job.

In a plot worthy of a good thriller, Republicans—on behalf of John Sununu, but likely without his knowledge—hired a phone calling center to jam the phone calls Democrats were making on Election Day to get out the vote and offer rides to the polls on behalf of Jeanne Shaheen. The Democratic Party and the firefighters' union had teamed up to make calls together on that day, but the problem was that they couldn't seem to make any calls at all. In fact, they were continually *receiving* phone calls that lasted only a few seconds, thus making it impossible for them to call out. It was estimated that nine hundred blocking calls came in over the course of the day, making it virtually impossible for the Shaheen camp to do their job. At one point, they could make no outgoing calls for a full hour and a half. Verizon was finally able to stop the madness and trace where the calls were all coming from—a call center in Idaho—but the damage was done. The Dems had been stopped in their tracks.

So who was behind it all? By February of 2003, a serious investigation was underway, and the first person in the vise was state Republican executive director Charles McGee. An ex-military guy, McGee had been the one who had initially dreamed up the idea of cutting off "enemy communications." He resigned his position, and in 2004 pleaded guilty to several charges in federal court. Also pleading guilty was political consultant Allen Raymond, who was found to have used over $15,000 from state Republican Committee funds to pay for the project. (Raymond closes his 2008 book, *How to Rig an Election: Confessions of a Republican Operative*, with a reminiscence about his stint in prison: "After ten full years inside the GOP, ninety days amongst honest criminals wasn't any great ordeal.")

McGee may have come up with the phone-jamming idea, but someone had to have put the whole plan in motion, and it turned out that longtime Republican political operative James Tobin was the culprit. It had come to light that there had been dozens of phone calls from Tobin to Ken Mehlman's Office of Political Affairs at the White House in the weeks before the 2002 election. By the time the New Hampshire incident caught up with him in 2004, Tobin was New England campaign chairman for the Bush–Cheney presidential campaign. James Tobin was indicted and convicted, but he appealed, and though it took him until 2009, his conviction was eventually reversed.

So did this electronic scam cost Jeanne Shaheen her first senatorial election? It's hard to say. But it has been said that it cost the RNC about $3 million to pick up James Tobin's legal fees—and that's one expensive phone bill.

JUDGES
& FIXERS

It certainly seems that judges and fixers should be on opposite sides of the bench, but that's not always the case. What these tales have in common are men who have used their power to get away with things that mere mortals never could. From no-shows to bribery, cronyism to financial improprieties, it's fair to say that history has often put the gavel in the wrong hands.

JOHN PICKERING

(1737–1805)

P olitical firsts are the stuff of history: JFK as the first
Catholic president of the United States, Barack Obama
as the first black man in the Oval Office. But to be the
first federal judge ever impeached? Not something you really
want on your CV. Worse yet, though by all reports Judge John
Pickering was at the very least a fool and a drunk, nothing he
did legally merited his getting the ax.

Pickering's first appointment was to the New Hampshire
Superior Court in 1790, where he rose to chief justice. Several
years later he became ill, and President George Washington
was persuaded to move him to the less strenuous United States
District Court for the District of New Hampshire. Pickering
recovered nicely, but after a few years, he began simply not

to show up for court. The consensus was that he was insane, and the judge was replaced for the remainder of the 1801 session. He was reinstated the next year, though, and appeared in court on the opening day of the session . . . and then promptly disappeared again. Pickering inspired a litany of complaints: unlawful rulings, arriving in court totally drunk, and taking God's name in vain.

It was obvious to all concerned that Pickering had to go, once and for all. Proving his insanity and the reports of his inebriated behavior seemed like an easy way to oust him—except that those offenses are not grounds for dismissal. Treason, bribery, and other high crimes and misdemeanors, yes, but Pickering's sins were none of those. That did not stop a congressional vote to impeach him, an act that may have been more illegal than anything the judge himself had tendered in his courtroom. Nearly everyone agreed that Pickering was unfit—but once the Senate starts throwing judges off the bench for that, what next?

MARTIN THOMAS MANTON

(1880–1946)

artin Manton was a man who could boast of two
notable firsts: in 1916, he was the youngest federal
judge in the United States, appointed at age thirty-six
by President Woodrow Wilson. He would go on to be the
first federal judge to be convicted of bribery. Perfect bookends
to a career on the bench.

Martin Thomas Manton graduated from law school at
Columbia University in 1901 and practiced privately in New
York until 1916, when he was tapped by President Wilson
to be a judge for the United States District Court for the
Southern District of New York. A mere two years later, he
got bumped up to the United States Court of Appeals for
the Second Circuit, a spot considered second only to a seat

on the Supreme Court. He very nearly made it to that to that bench as well, when the "Catholic seat" was vacated upon the retirement of Judge William R. Day in 1922—but a campaign to hold him off, led by past president and then Supreme Court chief justice William Howard Taft, succeeded.

So Judge Manton trundled on in New York City, likely loving the prestige of the judgeship but becoming more and more agitated at leaving his lucrative practice for a paltry judge's salary. The Wall Street crash in 1929 did not help; he later said, "I know there was a Depression. I felt it myself." It was around that time that Manton's reputation on the bench began to come under scrutiny. There had been those who thought he had been doing shady deals for years; finally, in 1939, District Attorney Thomas E. Dewey decided there was enough reason and evidence to investigate.

It turned out the judge had been selling decisions for quite some time, taking loans and bribes from various parties. Dewey brought charges that Manton and his corporations had taken $439,481 in bribes. In lieu of impeachment hearings, President Roosevelt asked for Judge Manton's resignation and got it on February 7, 1939, though the judge named a date three weeks later, which he suggested was more convenient. And then Manton then promptly departed for a sanitarium for "a severe nervous disorder."

When Judge Manton's case went to court, he made a last-gasp plea "to vindicate himself for the honor of the American judiciary" before the decision came down. Manton's lawyers joined in, saying that "from a broad viewpoint it serves no public policy for a high judicial officer to be convicted of a judicial crime. It tends to destroy the confidence of the people in the courts." Does it ever. In this case, that lack of confidence led to seventeen months in the federal pen.

In one of those terrible tricks of fate, Manton was convicted in the Federal Court House in Manhattan's Foley Square—the very building for which he had laid the cornerstone many years before. Should the reader still feel just a tinge of sadness for Judge Martin T. Manton, remember that it was he who decided to raise the New York City subway fare from five to seven cents.

In an interesting coda, a painting of Manton was unearthed many years later in a dusty courthouse storeroom by Judge Charles L. Brieant Jr., who recognized the scoundrel judge and had the portrait dusted off, cleaned, and hung in his office. Many who remembered Manton's legacy were disturbed, but Brieant was a bit of a jokester and cared not; he noted that it was a perfect reminder of the fallibility of judges. When Judge Brieant passed away in 2008 and the future of the Manton portrait was again in question, chief judge of the Second District Dennis Jacobs was firm. "If it has been a joke, it is now an old joke," he said. "I'm kind of hoping that Judge Manton will disappear."

ABE FORTAS

(1910–1982)

W hen someone says they have friends in high places, they
very rarely mean the president of the United States.
Or if they *say* that, it's very rarely true. But Abe Fortas
had an extremely close working relationship with President
Lyndon Baines Johnson, and in the end, it seemed to do him
more harm than good.

Abe Fortas had a fairly stellar career, rising to an appointment as an associate justice on the United States Supreme
Court. At Yale Law School, he had found an early mentor
in William O. Douglas, who would end up preceding him
to the Supreme Court. When Douglas went to Washington
to run the Securities and Exchange Commission, he brought
Fortas on as an adviser and helped him get a teaching job at

Yale. In the late 1930s through the mid-1940s, Fortas worked in various high-level government positions as undersecretary of the Interior for Franklin Delano Roosevelt, and later as a United Nations adviser for Harry Truman. It was in 1937 that Abe Fortas met Lyndon Baines Johnson through his boss, Secretary of the Interior Harold L. Ickes. LBJ would become the best friend a rising star could have.

In 1946, Abe Fortas teamed up with Thurman Arnold and started Arnold & Fortas, a law firm that later became the very prestigious Arnold & Porter. In 1948, LBJ was running for United States senator from Texas against that state's popular governor, Coke Stevenson. There was a kerfuffle about voting fraud, and Stevenson tried to have LBJ's name struck from the ballot—perhaps because it appeared that Johnson was in the lead. Fortas led the litigation on the case and all was well: Johnson entered the Senate, where he would remain extremely powerful until his ascendancy to the vice presidency in 1961. The Fortas-LBJ friendship was cemented, and all through the 1950s and '60s, Fortas remained a close adviser to Johnson on vital subjects of the day, including the war in Vietnam, civil rights, and the decision to empower the Warren Commission to investigate President Kennedy's assassination.

So when Johnson became president, he was determined to put his old friend on the bench of the United States Supreme Court. The manner in which he accomplished this coup, however, is still a questionable one. In order to free up a space on the bench, LBJ moved Supreme Court jurist Arthur Goldberg to a new job as ambassador to the United Nations. Sounds like a nice gig . . . if that's what Goldberg really wanted, and there's long been discussion about that. Goldberg said that the president had promised him he could negotiate the end of the Vietnam War, and that he would support a run for his presidency, which, if successful, would make Goldberg the first Jewish president. But it seemed that once he reached his United Nations office, LBJ forgot all about that.

So in 1965, Abe Fortas took the seat vacated by Arthur Goldberg. The president was certain that Fortas would give him a heads-up if problems arose on the question of constitutionality for any of his programs and plans for America's future. Whether that was true remains unknown, but Fortas did continue to work with LBJ on other matters during his time on the bench, including advising him on affairs both foreign and domestic and cowriting his 1966 State of the Union speech.

Abe Fortas's ride with LBJ wasn't over yet. In 1968, when Chief Justice Earl Warren announced his intention to retire—as soon as a replacement was found—Johnson wasted no time in nominating Fortas for the position. This rankled Republicans; they knew LBJ wanted to slide someone into Warren's seat—and then Fortas's, if it came to that—before the 1968 presidential election, which could possibly (and in fact, did) end in a Republican win. Then the filibustering began. Accusations during the Senate approval hearings came at Abe Fortas fast and hard; aside from the obvious charges of cronyism, there were allegations of financial conflicts in Fortas's extracurricular earnings.

It seemed that Justice Fortas had been paid $15,000 to gives a series of lectures during a summer session at American University. His salary at the Supreme Court was nearly

$60,000, so a 25% bump for the year was substantial. A job on the side looked unseemly at the time, and there were concerns about where the money was raised to pay Fortas. Approximately forty donors put money into the pot, many of them old law clients and friends of Fortas's. Senator Strom Thurmond and others brought up the question of whether or not Justice Fortas could remain objective if any of these donors' companies or interests were brought before the Supreme Court. (It bears noting here that today, ex-secretaries of state, most Supreme Court justices, and other high-ranking officials regularly collect speaker fees and have a net worth of several millions due at least in part to this practice.) It was plain that his naysayers were not going to give up: Fortas finally withdrew his name for consideration as chief justice. He remained on the bench as an associate justice, however, until another financial impropriety sprang up.

In 1969, it came to light that Fortas had yet another side job, this one with the Wolfson Foundation. Louis Wolfson was Fortas's old friend and former client who had been convicted on stock manipulation charges. It turned out that Wolfson had hired the Supreme Court justice to "advise" him. The deal was that Fortas would be put on a $20,000-a-year retainer that would last his lifetime; if he died first, the remainder of his wife's life as well. Nice work if you can get it, being paid for advice from beyond the grave. There was also talk that Fortas had promised to talk to LBJ about a presidential pardon for Wolfson, who had been jailed for some Wall Street hijinks and obstruction of justice. It was finally all to much—and other improprieties were in the wings—so at last Justice Abe Fortas resigned his seat on the Supreme Court and President Richard Nixon replaced him with Harry Blackmun. There would not be another Jewish Supreme Court justice until the appointment of Ruth Bader Ginsburg in 1993.

Abe Fortas tried to return to his old law firm, but they wouldn't have him. He started a new firm, Fortas & Koven, hanging out his shingle again, as he had first done in 1946.

G. HARROLD CARSWELL

(1919–1992)

H arrold Carswell was the political version of the kid who lived next door who your mom made you play with. You hated his politics, but gee, he was such a sad sack.

Initially, life went according to plan for Carswell. He grew up in Georgia, went on to Duke and then law school, and served in the navy in World War II. Along the way, he married a nice girl named Virginia. His first stumbling block was his campaign as a Republican for the Georgia legislature in 1948, which he lost. But the disappointment made Carswell realize he had a future elsewhere. He moved to Florida and started a law practice there. In 1953, was appointed U.S. attorney by President Dwight Eisenhower, whom Carswell had supported and campaigned for in the previous year's presidential election.

Within five years, Eisenhower bumped him up to his first judgeship for the United States Court for the Northern District of Florida. Then, just over a decade later, President Nixon offered him another seat, a new Federal Court position on the United States Court of Appeals for the Fifth Circuit. Carswell was doing well and had gone without a blip through the vetting process by the Senate for his last two judgeships. Which is why Harrold Carswell thought it would be no problem when, in 1970, he faced another vetting: he had been nominated to the biggest show of all, the United States Supreme Court.

Before he tapped Carswell for the job, President Nixon had nominated Clement Haynsworth of South Carolina, but niggling questions about some of Haynsworth's past rulings had put the brakes on his nomination. Nixon had wanted a conservative Southerner on the bench, and so he turned next to Carswell, expecting an easy and quick confirmation process. No one was going to say no to the president twice, after all. It just wasn't done (or at least it hadn't been done since Grover Cleveland was president).

The vetting had to be squeaky clean, though. Justice Abe Fortas had just stepped down over financial improprieties, and his successor would require a very close look to avoid any future issues. And that's just what Carswell got. Senator Ted Kennedy, eager to block a Republican seat on the Court, started in on him the very first day of the hearings, demanding from Carswell a list of his former clients from his law practice, including notes on which of them had appeared before him later in court. It was discovered that a whopping 58% of Judge Carswell's decisions had been overturned.

But it wasn't impropriety that brought Judge Carswell down; that was accomplished thanks to his racist views. A 1948 interview in Georgia newspaper the *Irwinton Bulletin* surfaced, from back when Carswell had first run for office. "I am a Southerner by ancestry, birth, training, inclination, belief, and practice. I believe that segregation of the races is proper and the only practical and correct way of life in our states," a younger Carswell had said. He continued, "I yield to no man, as a fellow-candidate, or as a fellow-citizen, in the firm vigorous belief in the principles of white supremacy, and I shall always be so governed." This was not the kind of Southerner Richard Nixon was looking for.

That about did it for Judge Carswell's chances, although a sad little quote from Senator Roman Hruska, one of the most conservative Republicans in the Senate at the time, did Carswell no favors. In a last-ditch attempt to buoy his chances at gaining the Supreme Court nomination, Hruska said: "Even if he was mediocre, there are a lot of mediocre judges and people and lawyers. They are entitled to a little representation, aren't they, and a little chance? We can't have all Brandeises, Frankfurters, and Cardozos."

Well, yes, in fact, what Americans hope for are as many Brandeises, Frankfurters, and Cardozos as possible. Both Hruska and Carswell were ridiculed, and Harrold Carswell's bid for the associate justice seat was defeated, 51 to 45. To add insult to Carswell's injury, Harry Blackmun finally won the appointment, and, as one of the most liberal judges on the Supreme Court bench, he authored 1973's *Roe v. Wade,* perhaps the most important piece of Supreme Court legislation since the landmark *Brown v. Board of Education* in 1954.

It was only a couple of weeks after the failed confirmation that Harrold Carswell resigned from his Florida judgeship and subsequently announced he was running for U.S. Senate from the Sunshine State—a surprise, since he held lifetime tenure as a judge. Evidently he still had that political bug more than twenty years after his first ill-fated campaign. This round went no better. Though he was now eager to bring down "the dark winds of liberalism" in the Senate that he felt had defeated him during the Supreme Court confirmations, he lost in the primary by a hefty two-to-one margin. It was back to lawyering for Harrold Carswell.

That long, arduous circle had to have taken its toll, but Carswell's troubles were not yet over. In 1976, he picked up an undercover cop in a mall where anonymous gay hookups were popular. They drove to a wooded area, where the former judge was arrested, charged with battery, and let go with a fine of $100. At the scene, he threatened suicide. Three years later, Carswell was beaten by a man whom he had asked to his hotel room.

G. Harrold Carswell died at the age of ninety-two, never having caught the brass ring.

LEE ATWATER
(1951–1991)

W hat about the behind-the-scenes guy? The one who lights the spark that fans the flame of political scandals? Lee Atwater was that go-to guy for the Republican Party during the 1970s and 1980s. He started his career with one of the most controversial and divisive politicians of the twentieth century, Senator Strom Thurmond of South Carolina, long an anti–civil rights advocate. Then in 1980, Atwater cut his teeth working for the South Carolina congressional race between Republican Floyd Spence and Democrat Tom Turnipseed.

From the start, Atwater's tactics were imaginative—and shockingly base. He plied some of his first shady career moves in the Spence-Turnipseed race. One was running a "push poll," which is the act of questioning a voter in order to influence them without employing any real data collection; its purpose is to disseminate rumors. Atwater's poll was designed to inform voters from the Deep South that Turnipseed was a member of the NAACP, and asking them their thoughts on that. But that was nothing compared to what came next. Having found that Turnipseed had undergone electroconvulsive therapy for depression as a teenager, he went for the jugular. At a Turnipseed press conference, a "reporter" planted by Atwater asked the congressional candidate whether he had ever had shock treatment. Atwater then told reporters that Turnipseed had been "hooked up to jumper cables."

Such dirty dealings bought Atwater a fast ticket to Washington. He worked for the Reagan administration under the auspices of Ed Rollins, who was at that time Reagan's political director. By the time the 1984 reelection campaign rolled around, Atwater had Rollins's old job and was also the campaign's deputy director, and he was hard at work doing what he did best: dirty tricks. This time, he focused on Democratic presidential candidate Walter Mondale's running mate, Geraldine Ferraro, digging up the old news that her parents were numbers runners in the 1940s and hinting that this fact, combined with Mrs. Ferraro's Italian heritage, implied Mafia connections.

Atwater's pièce de résistance came during the 1988 presidential campaign, when he went to work for George H. W. Bush. Atwater body-slammed Democratic opponent and Massachusetts governor Michael Dukakis by publicizing the Massachusetts weekend prison furlough program (which Dukakis did not institute) and a convicted murderer named

Willie Horton. Horton had been released for a weekend and never returned; he later went on to rape a woman. The campaign used the scandal as fodder for an anti-Dukakis ad. Atwater gleefully said, "By the time we're finished, they're going to wonder whether Willie Horton is Dukakis's running mate." Dukakis, of course, lost, and Lee Atwater went on to become chairman of the Republican National Committee in 1989.

Lee Atwater fell seriously ill just a year later and died at the age of forty of a brain tumor. During his illness, he converted to Catholicism and began to write to those he thought he had done wrong—one of whom was Tom Turnipseed. But opinions vary still on Atwater, even in death. Political consultant Mary Matalin, suspicious of his sudden religious conversion, insisted, "He was spinning right to the end." But Strom Thurmond perhaps wrote the bottom line: "He was a kingmaker."

SEX &
OTHER VICES

★ ★ ★

It is ironic that something that should be one of the great pleasures in life is the ruination of so many. And it seems that no industry tops the list in the sexual downfall category more than politics. Some with power feel it's a perk of the office; some get crazy in the candy store. But sex is only a part of it: there are plenty of other vices to go around. It's all fun and games until someone has too many, whether that means martinis, shots, lines, or bumps. Politics, like many businesses, is a world where socializing is just part of the job. But sometimes after-hours takes over all the hours; life falls away and the bottom drops out. Politics and bad behavior have long been comfortable bedfellows.

VICTORIA WOODHULL

(1838–1927)

F ree love activist. Wall Street shark. They were two sure-
fire ways to be an unpopular candidate in a presidential
election in 1872—and probably not much different now.
Add to that the fact that the candidate is a feisty, liberal
woman, and chances of success go right down the drain. But
run for president of the United States is exactly what Victoria
Woodhull did.

Victoria Claflin was never going to be an ordinary girl,
no matter when she was born. Her mother was a mystic, her
father a salesman of dubious patent medicines. She had only
three years of schooling, but even so, her teachers in Homer,
Ohio, could tell she was special. The family often worked
together to earn money, practicing healing, spiritualism, and

clairvoyance. Eventually the Claflins were run out of town—surprisingly not for any of their crazy sideshow antics, but for an arson insurance scam Mr. Claflin dreamed up. But Victoria would escape soon enough herself by marrying a doctor, Canning Woodhull, when she was fifteen. It would be about the last ordinary thing she would do.

The new Mrs. Woodhull's marriage wouldn't last. Her husband was a drinker and womanizer, and although she had two children by him, Victoria eventually called it quits. In 1866, she tried marriage again with Colonel James Harvey Blood, a Civil War veteran and himself a divorcée. That marriage lasted a decade, but in the midst of it, Woodhull (she kept her first husband's name) took on a lover for several years.

It's likely that her relationships—both marital and extracurricular—led Woodhull to become an advocate of the burgeoning free love movement. Far from the 1967 Summer of Love, which was primarily about carefree sexual experimentation, the earlier "free love" movement was an intellectual crusade that sought to separate love from the binds of both church and state. Marriage, divorce, and bearing children should be the right of any woman, Woodhull believed—when and as often as one chooses.

Woodhull's social views were only part of the profile that made her an unusual woman of her times. In 1870, she and her youngest sister, Tennessee "Tennie" Claflin, opened their own Wall Street brokerage firm, Woodhull, Claflin & Company. They had some help from Cornelius Vanderbilt, who not only believed in the sisters' acumen but also had been a customer of Victoria's as a medium (and quite possibly was Tennie's lover). Whatever his reasons for helping out the Claflin sisters, he was on the mark: they made a fortune. Reports have them making $700,000 in their first six weeks, which would be about $13 million today.

That Wall Street money helped the sisters start their next venture several months later and earned them a new moniker: "Queens of the Quill." *Woodhull & Claflin's Weekly* was first published in May of 1870, and it was considered quite radical ("Upward & Onward" was its motto), speaking to women's rights, free love, even vegetarianism. But mostly it was a vehicle to promote Victoria's most important agenda: a run for the presidency of the United States. Woodhull was a leading proponent of the women's suffrage movement, and she decided she was going to make Congress sit up and take notice.

On January 11, 1871, Victoria Woodhull became the first woman to address a congressional committee on any matter whatsoever. Woodhull's agenda was close to her heart: she meant to convince Congress that women already had the right to vote, via the new 14th and 15th amendments, which were adopted in 1868 among the Reconstruction Amendments. Accompanied by her sister suffragists Susan B. Anthony and Isabella Beecher Hooker, Woodhull argued that the new amendments implied that women had the right to vote. Few agreed with her, but she had gotten her foot in the door and made her point.

Woodhull announced her intention to run for president— whether women could vote for her or not—and on May 10, 1872, the Equal Rights Party nominated her in New York City, making her the first woman candidate for the office. (The party also nominated Frederick Douglass for vice president, though he never recognized or accepted the offer.) There wasn't much the government could do about Woodhull's entering the race, but they did devise a way to keep her out of the limelight on Election Day: they arrested her, Colonel Blood, and Tennie. *Woodhull & Claflin's Weekly* had written extensively about an affair between the extremely popular and respected Henry Ward Beecher and his alleged mistress, and so the trio was charged with "publishing an obscene newspaper" and spent a month in jail for this alleged misdemeanor. That was a sure-fire, albeit extreme, way to keep Woodhull away from the polls—and away from the press as well. Though later acquitted, the government had found a way to take Victoria Woodhull out of the picture, at least temporarily. The Equal Rights Party candidate did not receive any electoral votes, and any popular votes she received were never counted. Exhausted and defeated, Victoria Claflin Woodhull moved to England in 1876 and married yet again, becoming Victoria Woodhull Martin. There she began a new publication, *The Humanitarian*, which she ran until 1901.

As in the case of so many visionaries, the political world—and the world at large—were not ready for Victoria Woodhull, but she helped set the stage for so much to come. "I shall not change my course because those who assume to be better than I desire it," she once said.

Spoken like a true rebel.

DAVID IGNATIUS WALSH

(1872–1947)

For nearly half a century, David Ignatius Walsh served the people of Massachusetts in many capacities, from his first entrance into the political arena in the state legislature in 1900, to lieutenant governor, governor, and then nearly three decades as a United States senator until just a few months before his death in 1947.

Walsh's story was one of the typical Irish immigrant. He was number nine out of ten children born to parents who came over on the boat. His father made combs, and died when David was twelve; his mother carried the family by running a boarding house and likely nearly burst with pride when her son entered Holy Cross and went on to law school.

Before James Michael Curley, before the Kennedys, Walsh was the pol breaking down barriers for Irish-Americans in Bay State politics. A Democrat in a Republican stronghold, he fought for women's suffrage, child labor laws, and for working people like his own family. He was a fine orator, he worked hard, and he stood for what he believed in. He was also gay. If they were at all aware, Walsh's constituency ignored his sexuality; it was more of an open secret among his brethren in Washington, but they too remained fairly quiet about it and let him do his job. A *Time* magazine piece on him in 1929 spoke of his "dandified" outfits and his "small and well-shod" feet, and homed in on his socializing, the expensive hotel suite where he resided, and his love of the theater. Even FDR reportedly commented to cronies that "everybody knew" Walsh was homosexual, and told Senate Majority Leader Alben Barkley that a good military man (Walsh had never served; nor, for that matter had Roosevelt) would end such disgrace by shooting himself. Walsh and FDR had long been at odds; Walsh was considered an isolationist in Washington, and his Irish heritage made him wary of aligning with the British in World War II.

In 1942, David Walsh's quiet life in the closet ended with a roar. The *New York Post* named him in one of the juiciest sex scandals ever, in the discovery of what was described as a male bordello in Brooklyn (though the *New York Times*, Gray Lady that she is, called it a "resort"). The proprietor and some clients identified Walsh as a former client called "Doc," but the *Post*, in its continuing coverage, began to talk about a "Senator X," and eventually named Walsh as that man. Then the other shoe dropped: the "brothel" was supposedly also a hangout for Nazi spies, and suddenly Walter Winchell had dubbed it the "Swastika Swishery."

Several of Walsh's fellow senators came to his defense, including FDR pal Alben Barkley. The FBI's investigation did close down the "house of degradation" (as the *Post* insisted on calling it) and cleared David I. Walsh completely of anything the newspaper had reported about him. No charges were ever brought against him, but that hardly mattered; the damage to Senator Walsh's career was done. He still had four years left in his term, and he served them out. President Roosevelt even threw him a bone, asking Walsh to join him in public just a few days before the 1944 presidential election to campaign with him—hands across the divide for both of them.

Despite his family's pleadings, David Walsh ran one more time for the senate in 1946, but lost to Henry Cabot Lodge Jr., who, it must be said, ran a gentlemanly campaign with no moralistic finger-pointing. David I. Walsh, depressed and disappointed in the voters of Massachusetts, to whom he had devoted his life, died the following summer of a cerebral hemorrhage.

WILBUR MILLS

(1909–1992)

Much of Congressman Wilbur Mills's life—the majority, in fact—is stamped with good deeds, a fine congressional record, and, finally, redemption. But as in all downfalls, those years are never the dishy part of the story.

Mills was a Democrat from Arkansas, from a family of liberals. His father was a school superintendent who helped to integrate Wilbur's public school, which was the first one in the state to teach both black and white students. Valedictorian of his high school and salutatorian in college, young Wilbur then went on to Harvard Law School. And at last, in 1939 at age thirty, Wilbur Mills arrived in Washington.

He became an extremely powerful voice in Washington and remained in Congress for nearly four decades, from 1939 to 1977. Seventeen of those years were spent as the chairman of the House Ways and Means Committee. To this day, no one has held the chair longer. He helped develop Medicare, as medical aid for the poor was an early interest from back in his Arkansas days. In fact, Mills and Senator Ted Kennedy had also been working feverishly on the Kennedy-Mills universal health care reform bill in the summer of 1974, which Mills managed to get through the Ways and Means Committee with a 13–12 vote. With such a narrow margin, Mills was nervous about bringing the bill to the House floor—but that became a moot question just a few months later on the morning of October 9.

Wilbur Mills's life went to hell in a handbasket when his car was stopped by police at 2:00 A.M. for driving with no headlights on. He was drunk, his glasses were broken, and his face was all cut up. And he was in the company of a stripper—a stripper who jumped out of the car and into the Tidal Basin, in what the cops would later call a half-hearted suicide bid. But it gets juicier. Mills claimed she was a Washington neighbor, a Mrs. Annabel Battistella, originally of Argentina, and all that was true—but she was more famously known as Fanne Foxe, a dancer at the Silver Slipper, where she was known as the "Argentine Firecracker."

Wilbur had a further excuse about the whole evening, as reported in the *Washington Post*. "[My wife's] broken foot prevented our entertaining at home and she insisted I take our friends to a public place we had frequented before. This I did," he explained. "We then visited another place and after a few refreshments Mrs. Battistella became ill and I enlisted the help of others in our group to assist me in seeing her safely home." Since Mills looked beaten up and Battistella/Foxe ended up in a mental hospital, perhaps she should have asked for a better host.

Of course the real story was that Fanne and Wilbur had been canoodling for some time and that, according to people who saw them regularly at the Silver Slipper, altercations and arguments were far from unusual. But in those pre–social media days, no one had ever nabbed a surreptitious photo of them or reported any hanky-panky online. In fact, Mills managed to lay low for a few days after the arrest, claiming that the whole thing was a string of unfortunate circumstances—evidently brought on by "a few refreshments." (He ultimately holed up for a week.) And then, on November 4, Wilbur Mills won reelection with 60% of the vote.

It might have ended there, just a lone, suspicious, tawdry incident . . . but it didn't. When Fanne was playing a joint in Boston just a few weeks later, an obviously drunken Wilbur Mills toddled onstage, gave her a kiss, and then followed up with a press conference in the stripper's dressing room. Enough was enough for the Ways and Means Committee, and Mills was asked to step down as chairman.

To his credit, Wilbur Mills redeemed himself—personally, if not politically. He joined Alcoholics Anonymous, decided not to run for reelection in 1976, and went into private law practice. When he retired in 1991, he returned to Arkansas and established the Wilbur D. Mills Treatment Center. Not much more was heard about a universal health care reform bill until Hillary Clinton proposed one in 1993.

And the Argentine Firecracker? She eventually returned to South America. During a 1974 interview with Bill O'Reilly, she confessed a desire to go to medical school. And, who knows? Perhaps one can still make a private appointment with Dr. Fanne Foxe in Buenos Aires.

BETTY FORD

(1918–2011)

P resident-to-be Gerald Ford made a media splash as early
as the 1940s, working as a hunky model in his twenties,
even making the cover of steamy *Cosmopolitan* magazine
in 1942 in a painted portrait of a naval officer canoodling
with a model who was actually his then-girlfriend. But it
was Gerald's wife Betty who would became the wild card
during his administration and afterward, generating headlines of her own.

The Fords had ridden into the White House on the dirtiest
coattails possible after the Watergate scandal and the resignation of President Richard M. Nixon. Following an era of
secrecy that generated public distrust in the government, they
were determined to be open and honest. This extended to

their personal lives. When the First Lady was diagnosed with breast cancer in 1974, shortly after her husband took office, Mrs. Ford underwent a mastectomy as part of her treatment and immediately spoke openly about her operation. She was one of the first public figures to talk about the disease, and played an enormous role in bringing its discussion into the open.

Mrs. Ford did not stop there. Women's rights, marijuana use, sex (both premarital and between herself and her husband), abortion—it was all fodder for the First Lady. Some called her a political train wreck in the making, while others praised her honesty. Betty's vocal participation in politics resulted in *Time* magazine naming her a Woman of the Year for 1975.

But Betty's most important legacy was to come in the post–White House years. By 1978, a longtime addiction to alcohol and pills resulted in Betty's family staging an intervention; she agreed to enter a treatment facility. In 1982, several clean and sober years later, Mrs. Ford founded the Betty Ford Clinic, a treatment and recovery center for the chemically dependent. Almost immediately the "Betty" became a prestigious institution and cultural phenomenon that began to ease the stigma of substance abuse in the same way her announcement of breast cancer had years earlier.

Gerald Ford spent just 895 days in the Oval Office before losing his only campaign for the presidency to Jimmy Carter in 1976, but both Fords made their mark in history's pages.

JOHN G. SCHMITZ

(1930–2001)

t's got to be hard to get thrown out of the John Birch
Society, the über-conservative political group that enjoyed
its heyday during America's rabid anticommunist Cold
War days. So it says a lot about John G. Schmitz—the Orange
County, California, senator—that they were eager to toss him
to the curb for being too extreme.

Schmitz made his first appearance in the newspaper as a
young marine, in a story about how he'd chased off a man who
had been stabbing a woman. It was probably the last time he
ever made the news where every reader commended him for
his work. By 1964, already recognized as a particularly conservative candidate even in right-leaning Orange County, he
was elected to the California state senate. During his political

career, Schmitz won some and he lost some: in 1970, he went to Congress on a special election, got the next hitch on his own, then lost the primary in 1972, lost again when he ran in 1976, and then decided to return to the state senate, where he remained from 1979 through 1982. It was a checkered career.

In 1972, Schmitz decided it was time for the big show. Angry with fellow Orange County resident Richard M. Nixon for not supporting him in his congressional race, he decided to run against Nixon for president. He was a candidate on the American Independent Party ticket, working with the people who had put up Governor George Wallace as a presidential candidate four years earlier. John Schmitz pulled in over a million votes in the 1972 election, which sounds not so bad until one realizes it was even less than the other also-ran, George McGovern. At least McGovern had won one state.

By the early 1980s, John Schmitz's views and values had offended just about everybody, and the extreme right-wing Republican's political career came to a screeching halt. He was quoted as saying outrageous lines like, "I may not be Hispanic, but I'm close. I'm Catholic with a mustache." He called Martin Luther King Jr. "a notorious liar" and insisted that "Those who work ought to live better than those who don't." Schmitz's policies were no less outrageous. For starters, he was against sex education in the schools, but in favor of the right to carry loaded weapons. He was also staunchly pro life and vehemently homophobic.

Then, in 1981, the skies opened and the rain poured down. As a stunt at an anti-abortion lecture he gave, noted lawyer and feminist Gloria Allred presented Schmitz with a chastity belt. In retaliation, Senator Schmitz's staff wrote a press release (which Schmitz said he never read, although had ordered it to be written) entitled "Senator Schmitz and His Committee Survive Attack of the Bulldykes." It called Allred "a slick, butch lawyeress" and her supporters at the lecture "a sea of hard Jewish and (arguably) female faces." Gloria Allred slapped him with a suit for $10 million, which she settled five years later for $20,000 and an apology. She vowed to donate the money to those Schmitz had maligned, such as the National Council of Jewish Women, the Gay and Lesbian Community Service Center, and the California Abortion Rights Action League.

The next year, 1982, saw the end of Schmitz's political career and made his stance on anything remotely smacking of "family values" laughable. John Schmitz and his wife, Mary, had had seven children. But now along came Carla Stuckle, his mistress, who also had two children by him. Perhaps Schmitz's career could have been saved if he had fessed up and then gone ahead and did the right thing by apologizing to his family and his constituency, and supporting his love children. But, no: he admitted the children were his, but he insisted he had no financial obligation. Even the John Birch Society had had enough of him by then. That same year, they asked him to turn in his membership card.

Remarkably, Schmitz's wife, Mary, stayed with him through it all. But when Carla passed away several years later, the Schmitzes would not take John's out-of-wedlock offspring; they pawned them off instead to nationally syndicated astrologist, alleged psychic, and sometime presidential adviser Jeane Dixon. (She must have seen that coming, right?) And that was the end of John Schmitz's political career.

So he was out of politics, but not out of the headlines quite yet. In a wicked, wicked twist of fate, his daughter Mary Kay Letourneau made national news headlines in 1994, following an affair with her then twelve-year-old student, Vili Fualaau. John Schmitz passed away in 2001, and so the former congressman did not live to see the day when Mary Kay emerged from prison and married Vili, her "high school sweetheart." But the family values man may just have turned over in his grave.

BOB PACKWOOD

(1932–)

U nited States senator Bob Packwood came from a long line of politicians, dating back to 1857, when his great-grandfather, William H., was part of the Oregon Constitutional Convention. Packwood took up the family trade as an energetic Republican in his home state of Oregon, playing party politics and making a name for himself. In 1963, at the age of twenty-nine, he entered the Oregon House of Representatives, and just five years later—after a squeaker of a race with a longtime incumbent—he won the race for the United States Senate.

Packwood came to Washington as the youngest senator in town, a socially moderate Republican who supported civil rights, gun control, and legalized abortion, and won accolades from many women's groups, including Planned Parenthood and the National Women's Political Caucus. He and his wife, Georgie, were a popular breath of fresh air. Packwood worked tirelessly to ingratiate himself into the political system, and by 1985 he replaced Daniel Patrick Moynihan as chairman of the powerful Senate Committee on Finance. He was now one of the most powerful men in Washington, but he was also a massive drinker. Before his 1980 senate campaign, Georgie finally talked him into seeing a therapist about it. He returned from the appointment and reportedly declared, "I am not an alcoholic. I have what is called a drinking problem." So the charade continued.

More than a decade later, in 1992, it all began to come apart—and Packwood certainly wouldn't be getting any more kudos from women's groups. Instead, he was getting hit with charges of sexual harassment. Many of his victims were staff members or lobbyists; the former often just left his employ to avoid the problem. The weird thing about the allegations that were coming to light is that Packwood really didn't seem to understand what the problem was. He'd say awkward things like, "I'm apologizing for the conduct that it was alleged that I did." It was the non-denial denial, as Woodward and Bernstein would have said.

Of all the accusers, the worst indictment of Packwood's bad behavior came from Packwood himself. We know plenty about what Packwood thought *and* did during those years, because, of all things, he kept a diary— a diary that sounded like it belonged to a teenage girl. In 1993, that diary was subpoenaed by the Senate Ethics Committee, and by 1995, excerpts appeared in every major newspaper across the country. Just a sample of his extremely odd and unsettling grasp of sexual boundaries:

Grabbed Tracy Gorman behind the Xerox machine today and she got a little pissed. What's the big deal? I was smiling while I did it. She made this big stink about it and it took me about two hours and a couple of thousand dollars to calm her down. I have one question—if she didn't want me to feather her nest, why did she come into the Xerox room? Sure, she used that old excuse that she had to make copies of the Brady Bill, but if you believe that, I have a room full of radical feminists you can boff. She knew I was copying stuff in there. I had my jacket off and my sleeves rolled up, revealing the well-defined musculature of my sinewy arms which are always bulging with desire. I know what she wanted. This didn't require a lot of thought.

Worse yet, it came to light that in the time between the start of his misconduct investigation and the release of his diary to the committee, Packwood had gone back and changed and even deleted portions of the record. Even crazier (if possible), he confessed in the diary about making the edits. This tortuous political drama went on until 1995, when Packwood resigned under immense pressure from the Senate. (Georgie, by the way, had divorced him at last in 1991.)

It seems that power doesn't die, however. In 1998, Bob Packwood founded the Sunrise Research Corp., a lobbying firm with high-rolling clients like the AFL-CIO, United Airlines, and the Court of Ohio. He still spends half the year in Washington, the other half in his beloved Oregon.

MARION BARRY
(1936–2014)

I f anybody holds the record for committing political suicide,
it has got to be Marion Barry. He also may hold the record
for resurrections. Marion Barry had nine lives—at least
political ones—for sure.

Born in Mississippi during the Great Depression, Barry
was the son of sharecroppers in the last days of that post-
Reconstruction way of life. As a kid, he picked cotton,
delivered newspapers, and became an Eagle Scout. In
college, he was the chapter president of the NAACP and
became the very first president of the burgeoning Student
Nonviolent Coordinating Committee (SNCC) in 1960.
He then earned a master's degree in organic chemistry,
worked with Martin Luther King Jr., and started his

doctoral degree. But the pull to continue work in the civil rights movement won out, and he quit school to continue his work with SNCC full-time.

In 1965, Barry and his wife moved to Washington, D.C., and though the marriage wouldn't last, his love for the city would. It was there that Barry found his home. Like many political careers, Barry's started with his school board race. When Washington passed a home rule law in 1973, which allowed D.C. to elect its own leaders—including a city council and a mayor for the District of Columbia—Barry jumped at the chance and won a seat on the very first city council. His political career wasn't to go entirely smoothly, however: Councilman Barry was shot by a member of a rogue Muslim group in 1977. The bullet lodged in his chest, inches from his heart. But he recovered and threw his hat into the mayoral race, becoming Washington, D.C.'s second mayor on January 2, 1979. He would go on to serve four terms from 1979 until 1999, with one notable gap from 1991 to 1995. That four-year gap was where some of the bloom came off the Marion Barry rose.

The mayor, you see, had a penchant for drugs and partying. When the rumors of cocaine use first started to float around D.C., Barry shrugged them off. "I may not be perfect," he went so far to admit, "but I am perfect for Washington." His team took that quote, and with a little tweak turned it into a winning campaign slogan: "He may not be perfect, but he's perfect for D.C." Even when he was breaking the law, it seemed like the guy could do no wrong.

But Barry continued to get into deeper trouble. On January 18, 1990, he was nabbed in an FBI sting operation that found him smoking crack in a hotel room. His companion was his former girlfriend Rasheeda Moore, who was at that time working as an FBI informant. (Barry was then married to the third of his four wives.) Though Barry insisted he'd been set up, he served jail time for the crack arrest. Still, within months of his 1992 release from prison, the once and future mayor was running for the D.C. Council again, back where it all began. In 1995, he won a fourth term running the District, earning himself the moniker as Washington, D.C.'s "Mayor for Life."

But Barry's troubles were far from over. In 2002, his car was stopped and traces of pot and coke were found. (Barry insisted they were planted.) In 2005, he was put on probation for not filing or paying taxes for several years. In September of 2006, he ran a red light, and when a breathalyzer proved inconclusive, he refused a urine test; he was given a ticket both for running the red light and for refusing the urine analysis. In 2009, he was arrested for stalking an ex-girlfriend. He blamed another traffic violation in 2014 on adverse effects of his diabetes. He was also heard making racist remarks against both Asians and Polish people.

His record was far from perfect; in addition to his personal issues, Barry was also accused over the years of overspending, cronyism, and questionable government contracts. But upon his death, the *New York Times* said, "Admirers saw him as a Robin Hood who gave hope to poor black residents." His was also one of the greatest underdog stories in history: a poor, hard-working young black man in pre–civil rights America who broke every barrier he faced and played an important part in making change in a major city. The hubris that got him to the top of the heap may have also been his downfall. But his accomplishments are unquestionable. This was a man who, when he went back to his council seat in 1994 after being imprisoned, pulled in *95% of the vote* in the general election. He still held that seat when he died at seventy-eight in 2014. Marion Barry couldn't lose for winning.

GOVERNMENT HIJINX

There are so many facets to the government scandal: greed, bribery, payback, payoffs, bad decisions, poor planning, and often just plain stupidity. Most often it's a bad recipe: too many people and a dollop of bad communication, stirred up with greed and avarice. Good luck trying to keep that a secret. It would be naïve to think that politics exists without treachery. Wherever power resides, the threat of its misuse is never far. The human condition makes it a safe bet that someone, somewhere, is looking for a way to take advantage of the other guy.

JAMES WOLFE RIPLEY

(1794–1870)

J ames Wolfe Ripley is the perfect example of how you
don't actually have to be an elected politician to incite
grave and immense political repercussions

A graduate of West Point's class of 1814 (he was pushed
through in just over a year, as there was a need for officers in
the continuing War of 1812), Ripley was always dedicated to
the military. He came out of the academy with a commission
as second lieutenant of artillery. A brigadier general in the
Union Army during the Civil War, Ripley enjoyed a reputation as a forward-thinking artillery expert in the early days
of his career. Perhaps it's no coincidence that he was born in
Connecticut near Hartford, close to the Colt, Winchester,
and Sharps firearms companies that have long been integral
to the Nutmeg State's economy and the nation's gun business.

For the next several decades, Ripley had a long and storied career as an artillery officer at Sackets Harbor, in upstate New York, before moving on to Fort Moultrie, South Carolina (at the time of that state's threat of nullification), then on to command Kennebec Arsenal in Maine and Springfield Armory in Massachusetts. In 1861, during the Civil War, the 66-year-old Ripley was given the post of brigadier general and then was subsequently appointed chief of ordnance for the army. Certainly his experience warranted the position, but once installed he made what many historians say was a crucial mistake in the Civil War.

Perhaps it was his large-scale weaponry background that caused him to miscalculate, but Ripley refused to order the purchase of breech-loading rifles for the soldiers on the ground, opting instead to save money and use the existing stockpile of less-accurate smoothbore muskets and other weaponry that the army already had on hand. (The breech-loader had a considerably faster reloading time.) At the same time, the Confederate Army was consistently buying modern weaponry from European countries, and though their loss in the war was inevitable, most historians agree that the North's lack of quality guns added up to two additional horrific, deadly years of warfare.

Because of his obstinacy toward the introduction of the newer rifles, Ripley was forced out of his job as chief of ordnance in 1863—smack in the middle of the Civil War. He was given a position as inspector of armament of forts along the New England coast and allowed to remain in uniform until his retirement in 1869, a time he almost surely spent wondering if he had done the right thing and served the country he loved in the best way possible after all.

THE PETTICOAT AFFAIR

(1830–1831)

There's the old saw about a woman being behind every great man, but what about love, lust, and moral superiority setting Washington afire with scandal and bringing down a slew of politicians? It happened in the 1830s, and all because of just *one* woman.

That woman—who was really just a young girl when our story begins—was named Peggy O'Neale. Bright, educated, witty, and beautiful, she had already begun to turn heads as a teenager when she worked at her family's boarding house and tavern in Washington, D.C. She sang, played the piano, served some drinks, and entertained the guests—all of whom were men. They were a pretty classy lot, though, and even from a young age, it's likely Peggy had her eye on moving up in the world. Politicians, generals, and such were Franklin House guests, and by the time she was fifteen years old, Peggy already had one botched elopement under her belt. It didn't take long for her to get back in the game, though: in 1816, when she was seventeen, Peggy married John B. Timberlake, a 39-year-old navy purser, who must have thought he'd died and gone to heaven.

Timberlake had problems, though—deep financial woes. He returned to sea to try to earn some money and rectify them, but he became ill and died from a heart condition (or committed suicide because his wife had been unfaithful; reports differ). Either way, while he was at sea, Mrs. Timberlake had been keeping company with Senator John Eaton, a friend of hers and her husband's. They married soon after Timberlake's death, to no one's great surprise—there had been much speculation about an affair between the now-married Eatons back when Timberlake was still at sea. One Washington wag said what was on many minds: "Eaton has just married his mistress, and the mistress of eleven doz[en] others!"

It was true that, at that point, Peggy had quite a reputation. She was extremely popular with important men around Washington. With the ladies of Washington, not so much. She had stepped out of bounds in many ways, and the other wives were far from pleased. In particular, they objected to what they saw as her insufficient mourning for her late husband. Also, Peggy knew how to talk business with men, unheard of in the early 1800s.

Peggy pushed on, undeterred by the whispers. She and her husband ran with a fairly exclusive group fellow politicians, and in their inner circle was a senator named Andrew Jackson. Jackson thought Mrs. Eaton had a truly great brain, and he was heard saying that Peggy was "the smartest little woman in America." But the combination of her party-girl past and chummy relationship with Washington's elite set the local ladies' teeth on edge. In 1829, when Andrew Jackson took up residence at 1600 Pennsylvania Avenue, he appointed John Eaton as his secretary of war. It's common enough for citizens to carp and disagree with a president's cabinet choices, but this time, it was closer to home: the cabinet wives took a stand against the appointment and the Eatons themselves.

Advisers and friends had warned the new president that these women would form a social and political barricade for Mrs. Eaton. President Jackson's angry response was: "Do you suppose that I have been sent here by the people to consult the ladies of Washington as to the proper persons to compose my cabinet?" Perhaps he should have, as the snubbing got so out of hand that it actually changed history.

Floride Calhoun, wife of the vice president, John C. Calhoun, took charge as the ringleader of the mean girls. Initially, the other cabinet members and Jackson supporters brushed off the grumbling and scoffed at the ridiculous possibility that political wives could have any effect at all on their husbands' careers. But it just didn't stop—Floride Calhoun would receive a visit from Mrs. Eaton, but never return one, as was the socially (and in this case, politically) correct thing to do. And eventually, the other cabinet wives did the same.

Aside from his real fondness for Peggy Eaton, President Jackson had a personal understanding of what the Eatons were going through; when he had married his own wife, Rachel

Donelson Robards, they had both been under the impression that she was divorced. But the divorce apparently had not gone through by the time of their marriage, which was terrific fodder for the press when Jackson made his run for the White House. When Rachel died before her husband took the oath of office, he was heartbroken, and he believed the gossip and pressure she had been under had contributed to her death.

By 1830, what became known as the "Petticoat Affair" was in full swing. Secretary of State Martin Van Buren saw the dissent and damage it was causing in the Democratic Party; Van Buren was also the only bachelor in the Cabinet, so he had a less emotional view of the goings-on than the other secretaries. And just maybe he had an agenda for himself. Van Buren convinced John Eaton to step down as secretary of war, and then resigned himself. President Jackson had had enough and demanded the resignation of the rest of the cabinet except for the postmaster general, William T. Barry. By 1831, the president had assembled a new group of top advisers, which quickly became known as the aptly named "Kitchen Cabinet." John Calhoun (and his meddlesome wife) were promptly dumped from the 1832 presidential ticket, and Martin Van Buren happily accepted the spot as vice president. By 1837, he was settled in the Oval Office himself. Calhoun went on to the United States Senate, and John Eaton moved on to become governor of the Florida Territory and then was appointed ambassador to Spain.

But whatever happened to poor Peggy? John Eaton died in 1856, and, this time, Peggy waited a very proper three years before marrying her third husband. But the scandal this time wasn't in the timing of her marriage, but in her choice of spouse: Antonio Gabriele Buchignani, her third husband, was her granddaughter's Italian dancing teacher, who just happened to be nineteen to Peggy's fifty-nine years old. Whatever inroads Mrs. Eaton had made back into high society after the Petticoat years were dashed, and she was a pariah once more. And by 1866 Antonio had managed to talk a desperate Peggy into signing over everything she had to him, including nineteen homes and a large farm in what is now Dupont Circle. Then he ran off to Italy with his wife's seventeen-year-old granddaughter and married her when Peggy finally granted him a divorce. In 1879, Margaret O'Neale Timberlake Eaton Buchignani died in poverty in Washington, D.C., back in the town that had brought her down.

THE WHISKEY RING

(1875)

U lysses S. Grant's presidency was fraught with scandal, much of it the fallout from terrible human resources practices. The man had an uncanny talent for hiring scoundrels, and throughout his presidency, they seemed to come and go from his administration. Grant managed to win a second term, but, as time has passed, the breadth and depth of corruption during his administration has considerably tarnished his reputation and that of his White House reign.

One of the biggest bombs of the Grant years was the Whiskey Ring in 1875. Like many great scams, it was simple— so beautifully simple. It was centered around the distilleries of St. Louis, though the same type of fraud was also happening in other cities around the country on a lesser scale. Government agents—whose job it was to tax the whiskey that was being produced in the United States—would ignore a percentage of the liquor being made and take a kickback from the distillers for each bottle ignored. Distillers were happy to give a smaller cut to agents than their tax on each bottle would have been, and, in this way, everybody won. (Well, everyone except the government.) At the center of the St. Louis shenanigans was former Civil War general John McDonald, a Grant crony who had been awarded the position of regional superintendent for the Internal Revenue Service. The collectors often declared that this skim was being put to good use, claiming that it went to funds to reelect President Grant, and, though some of the money did go to that purpose, historians question whether Grant actually was ever aware of the wrongdoings. The majority of the millions swindled from 1870 to 1875 went directly into shady pockets.

Another of the central Whiskey Ring characters was President Grant's own much-trusted personal secretary, Orville E. Babcock. Grant was much impressed with Babcock's military career and held him in high regard, but Benjamin Bristow, the president's new secretary of the treasury (the old one, William A. Richardson, had to be let go due to yet *another* Grant administration scandal) soon realized that Babcock had a hand in the whiskey tax avoidance mess. Without President Grant's permission or knowledge, Bristow gathered a group of secret agents and raided distilleries in several cities on May 10, 1875. It was a smashing success, with 110 convictions by the time all the trials ended, and over $3 million recovered for Internal Revenue coffers. One might think President Grant would be thrilled, but it pierced his old-boy-network heart something awful.

Earlier in the year, Bristow had informed Grant that it appeared that Babcock was knee-deep in the Whiskey Ring, and a saddened Grant reluctantly told the treasury secretary to "let no guilty man escape." But when it came time to indict Babcock, Grant flip-flopped and cooled on the investigation. The consensus was that not only was he disappointed about Babcock's part in the affair, but he also felt that it could point to his own involvement. So to everyone's shock—and surely the dismay of many on the White House staff—Grant gave a deposition in 1876 in which he proclaimed that he was certain of Orville Babcock's innocence. In fact, he was so certain, he put Babcock right back in his old job as private secretary.

Babcock's legal woes were far from over. In 1876, he was indicted for involvement in another White House scandal, the Safe Burglary Conspiracy, a plot involving corrupt D.C. contractors. Again he was acquitted, but by now the public tide against him was just too much, and he resigned from his White House role. An ever-faithful Ulysses Grant took care of him, however, by giving his old friend yet another chance: Babcock was appointed inspector of lighthouses at Mosquito Inlet, Florida. (Way to keep someone out of the public eye, USG!) There Orville Babcock met a tragic end at the age of forty-eight, when a boat he was on capsized.

THE TEAPOT DOME SCANDAL

(1921–1924)

I t's fascinating to ponder what history—and politics—would have been like if today's technology and the media existed back in yesteryear. The world certainly would have known about Franklin D. Roosevelt's polio, and likely his every doctor's visit. JFK's philandering would have been common knowledge and tabloid fodder; it may have even squelched his presidential bid. When we consider the first big modern-day political scandal, we think of Watergate, the Washington hijinks from which all "-gates" flow. But if we could look into the past through a big-screen TV, we'd all be glued to the twists and turns of the very messy Teapot Dome Scandal.

The incident had nothing to do with tea or with a vaulted ceiling, but with a bribery scandal at a Wyoming oil field named Teapot Dome, after a nearby rock formation. The United States Navy was beginning to see that the future of fueling ships was not going to be with coal, but oil, so they approached Congress about putting aside oil-rich Wyoming land for fuel reserves. These reserves were not to be used unless an oil emergency threatened. Though it all went down in the early 1920s, the Teapot Dome scandal is a very contemporary story; essentially, government contracts were being given without opening the bidding to everyone. The hitch is that in this instance, it was perfectly legal under the Mineral Leasing Act of 1920. But it's the timeless money-under-the-table aspect that brought shame to the Warren G. Harding White House.

Greed, of course, was at the center of the scandal. The huge Wyoming oil reserve was transferred from the navy to the Department of the Interior and Harding pal Secretary Albert B. Fall, and then Fall in turn leased the rights on the down low to Harry F. Sinclair of Sinclair Oil (the dinosaur-logoed gas stations). It was all above board except for the financial compensation Fall began to receive. Chief among these was a no-interest loan from Edward L. Doheny, another oilman who reaped oil reserve rewards. When it was discovered, tempers flared and tales were tattled, and soon the Senate Committee on Public Lands was looking into the situation, led by Senator Robert M. La Follette Sr., whose suspicions escalated when his office was broken into. But it was the unpaid Doheny "loan" that brought Secretary Fall to his knees, and he was convicted of accepting bribes, thus becoming the first Cabinet member to be convicted while working in the White House, though it was several years before he was sent up the river.

As for President Harding, he died in 1923 on a cross-country goodwill trip, an attempt to meet the people and clean up the image of corruption he'd managed to clothe himself in during just over two years as president. There was talk that Harding was poisoned by his wife for his philandering, or even that he committed suicide in the wake of his scandal-filled tenure. Congestive heart failure was the real culprit, but political wags have long asserted that Harding was lucky to die when he did: the alternative may have been impeachment. That's some Sophie's Choice.

ABSCAM

(1978–1980)

I t seemed like everyone was in on it. Everybody wanted a piece of the action.

It was a sting called Abscam, an FBI ploy that eventually brought down dozens of politicians between 1978 and 1980. The word Abscam stood for—depending on who you ask— "Arab scam" or "Abdul scam" (named after the fake company, Abdul Enterprises, that the FBI invented for the operation). Oddly, the entire idea started as a white-collar crime inquiry under the wing of FBI bureau supervisor John Good, who had recently been moved from Manhattan out to Hauppauge, New York. Trying to beef up the investigations taking place in the much sleepier Long Island office, Good oversaw the day-to-day dealings of the project, which was run by assistant director Neil

J. Welch and Thomas P. Puccio from the Department of Justice. And if this sounds a lot like the Hollywood blockbuster *American Hustle*, well, that's because truth is stranger than fiction. Much of that movie was based on the actual Abscam scandal.

Stolen art and theft were what Abscam was designed to concentrate on; local prosperous businessmen were their marks. At the center of the dupery was an extremely colorful con man named Mel Weinberg, who had been pulling stunts on people since he was a kid (including selling socks without feet as a street vendor). Weinberg was about to go to prison when the FBI approached him to help them do what he did best: take money from unsuspecting people. If he helped them, Weinberg would get no jail time, and he jumped at the chance. And so he and the FBI set up a fake Middle Eastern company called Abdul Enterprises and put $1 million in a bank account. Two FBI employees posed as the owners, Arab sheikhs named Kambir Abdul Rahman and Yassir Habib. Their story was that they had millions to invest in the United States and needed some guidance. When one customer suggested that the sheikhs might enjoy investing the gaming business in Atlantic City, the FBI ploy turned political.

The first politician Weinberg and the FBI pulled into their web was Camden, New Jersey, mayor Angelo Errichetti—and the mayor turned out to be the perfect target. The mayor couldn't be more helpful. In a 1981 *60 Minutes* interview with Mike Wallace, Weinberg recalled, "He would get into any crooked deal. He would bring up some real crazy deals to us. I mean, he wanted to get into counterfeit money. He wanted to give us the Port of Camden for narcotics. Anything that was dishonest, he wanted to do." Bingo.

Errichetti helped set the Abscam gang up with other politicians (for a cut, of course) who were willing to ease the way
to getting casino licenses and permits or to help the "sheikhs"
procure immigration papers for friends of Abdul Enterprises.
For a price, a lot of elected officials were more than willing to
help out. In the end, six congressmen and one United States
senator were convicted, as well as the ever-helpful Errichetti,
some members of the Philadelphia City Council, and even
an Immigration and Naturalization Service employee. By the
time the sting was over, more than $400,000 had been taken
in bribes and payoff money by government employees.

The entire Abscam circus was made for the media. The
hidden cameras that recorded the transactions with the politicians is what made the prosecutors nervous and the defendants'
lawyers outraged. It was the first time hidden camera videotapes
had been used at trial showing elected officials accepting bribes.
The men were easy marks and couldn't wait for the money-
for-favors rewards. Weinberg told *60 Minutes* that Congressman
Raymond Lederer of Pennsylvania chortled, "I'm no Boy
Scout!" And Congressman Richard Kelly of Florida told them,
"If you knew how poor I was, you'd cry for me." (Later on, in
a related movie moment, real-life FBI undercover agent Joseph
Pistone—known to the New York Mafia as Donnie Brasco and
played by Johnny Depp in the eponymous movie—nearly got
made when he used a yacht named *The Left Hand* for a party
venue, and it was recognized by a mobster pal as the same boat
the FBI used for an Abscam meet.)

Soon Abscam was the highlight of the nightly TV news.
The public loved the drama, and the legal system loved the
tapes. Though all the trials (which were each conducted

separately) had a lawyer objecting to the video on the basis of government entrapment, the videos were indeed used—and helped clinch the conviction every time.

There's an interesting little coda to everything Abscam. Remember FBI agent John Good, who helped start it all? In 2014, Good flew to South Dakota to campaign for Larry Pressler, who at the age of seventy-one ran—and lost—an open United States Senate seat. Good had never forgotten Larry Pressler; he was the only Congressman approached by the Abscam crew who had refused a bribe.

... AND PLAIN OLD RANDOM NUTTINESS

★ ★ ★

There are some scandals that seem insane, and then there are others that seem completely inexplicable—even in the wild world of American politics. Just when you think you've seen it all, someone drops onto the scene who defies all expectations and breaks all the rules. They may end up making more headlines than legislation, but take a close look, because these are the stories that make America great.

MURRAY HALL

(c. 1840–1901)

Murray Hall was a friend of Tammany Hall, known by all, well respected, and a popular man about-town for many years. He had the ear of the big boys, but he never ran for office himself, seemingly satisfied as captain of his election district in Greenwich Village. In those Tammany days past, many were called "politicians" though they did not hold an elected office. Hall was such a man, known as a "ward heeler," whose job it was to get constituents to the polls on Election Day however he could—whether it took threats, a few dollars, or a smack in the head. Any cronies who wondered why Murray Hall had never run for office himself got their answer when they read Hall's obituary in the *New York Times* on January 18,

1901: Murray Hall had died of breast cancer. Murray Hall was a woman and always had been.

Hall was "passing," a term most often used regarding blacks who wanted others to think they were white, usually in order to attain a higher social status and influence. But there was a time when another type of passing was happening under the radar, on the *very* down low. At the dawn of the twentieth century, particularly in metropolitan areas where women realized they were as smart as men but couldn't succeed like men solely because of their gender, they started "passing" as men. Possibly the most famous of these women was Murray Hall.

She was born Mary Anderson, in Govan, Scotland, around 1840. Mary was orphaned, moved to Edinburgh, and eventually set sail for New York City in the mid-1870s in her dead brother's clothes. She became Murray Hall during that voyage and never looked back. People remember Hall having a wife when he first arrived in Manhattan, but it appears she left him eventually, tired of his flirtations with other women. Hall opened an employment agency and acted as a bondsman in Greenwich Village. By the time he moved to a new apartment nearby, there was a new Mrs. Hall with him named Celia and an adopted daughter named Minnie. Father and daughter were very close, and when Celia passed away in 1898, Minnie was his joy and comfort.

Hall spoke with a high voice and was effeminate in appearance. He dressed in clothes that were large enough to disguise any hint of a womanly shape and wore custom shoes, as his feet were so tiny. But regardless of his skullduggery, Murray Hall was definitely a Tammany Hall insider, helping to keep the wheels of this Democratic übermachine greased. He was indeed a man among men, and his Tammany Hall buddies (and the rest of New York's politicos and high society) never questioned his identity for a minute. Not until the day Hall died, that is. Then the fur did fly.

The *New York Times* outed Murray Hall in its obituary. Deeming him a "man about town, bon vivant, and all-around good fellow," the paper also captured the reactions of acquaintances who were learning the news for the first time. One friend said, "So he's a woman, eh? Well, I've read of such characters in fiction, but if it's true, Hall's case beats anything in fact or fiction I can recall." Another said simply, "During the seven years I knew him I never once suspected that he was anything other than what he appeared to be."

The biggest shock may have been for Hall's daughter, Minnie. Celia Hall carried Murray's secret to her grave, and Minnie was learning about the revelation for the first time. "The poor girl is terribly shocked over the disclosure," the *Times* said of Minnie. "She said she had always believed her foster father was a man, and never heard her foster mother say anything that would lead her to suspect otherwise." At twenty-two years old, Minnie was Murray's sole heir and inherited about $10,000.

At his funeral, Murray Hill was buried in a dress, which may well have been the first one he'd worn in three decades. Upon his death, there are reports that a proposal was put forth requiring that the men of Tammany Hall wear whiskers of some sort. A bit of an identifier, just in case.

Murray Hall, née Mary Anderson, had lived over thirty years as a man, creating a life complete with power, privileges, and entitlement in a country that would not even ratify a woman's right to vote for nearly another two decades.

YETTA BRONSTEIN

(?–?)

Yetta Bronstein was smart, honest, fair, and devoted to the American Way. She was no-nonsense. She had no criminal past. In fact, what she stood for made a lot of sense when she ran for president in 1964—a race she lost, as she herself admitted, "in a landslide."

Mrs. Bronstein made perfect sense. "It is time for the country to have a mother," she insisted. "If a mother was in the White House, we would look to the presidency with more respect." She proposed "plain talk" proposals, such the abolishment of income taxes in favor of each member of the family weighing in on or before April 15th and paying $5.00 per pound, including pets. Her platform included some campaign promises and ideas that were popular then and would likely be appreciated by the American public in a candidate today.

Mrs. Bronstein's White House bid, on the Best Party ticket, boasted a straightforward, catchy slogan: "Vote for Yetta and things will get betta!" There were accompanying flyers, buttons, media coverage, and a campaign poster with Yetta's picture on it. But, despite a fair amount of media coverage of her campaign throughout the 1964 presidential race, no one ever saw the candidate in person.

No one ever saw her because Yetta didn't actually exist. It turned out that Yetta was a hoax, revealed at last in 1966, before she got too involved in her candidacy for the 1968 presidential election. She was the creation of Alan Abel—who bills himself as a "professional media hoaxer"—and his wife Jeanne. It was Jeanne who did the hundreds of newspaper and phone interviews, portraying a Jewish mother from the Bronx. The photo of Yetta used in her campaign materials was actually Alan's mother, Ida. And still, like any savvy politician, Yetta went on to write a book: *The President I Almost Was,* published in 1966, a memoir of her presidential dreams. Vintage copies are still available online.

Yetta Bronstein did not go gently into that good night. In a letter to Barack Obama in 2009, she offered the president a few of her proposals, "free of charge":

- Take Congress off salary and put them on straight commission
- Charge $5,000 for a marriage license and $5.00 for a no-fault divorce

- Employ a mental detector in the White House, as well as a metal detector
- National bingo
- Truth serum in the Senate drinking fountain

Oh, Yetta, we hardly knew ye.

ACKNOWLEDGMENTS

Without the terrible and colorful side effects that political careers hold dear—embezzling, adultery, castration, dueling, assault and battery, drunkenness, and, very possibly, murder—just to name a few—there would be no book. Those who hold public office are also in the public eye, and their bad behavior has provided their constituents with endless angst, distrust, and yes, even amusement. So I need to acknowledge all the politicians I've written about here, and countless more not included. I say acknowledge, because I can't *thank* them for taking advantage of the voters' trust. They have broken the law and often our hearts . . . but hopefully with the benefit of hindsight (sometimes centuries of it) their tales make for great reading.

I can, however, thank Iris Blasi and Claiborne Hancock at Pegasus Books for having the vision to see that these stories make for a fascinating respite in the present-day American political scene, especially during a presidential election year. They were on board immediately, realizing that history is often entertainment and that there's no better time than now for a little of that. Also a bow to jacket designer Michael Fusco-Straub, who worked so hard to convey the span of American history and got it so right.

And of course a tip of the hat to my agent Chris Tomasino, who keeps me sane and on course—and is a grand supporter and friend to boot.

And lastly I want to acknowledge the power of the vote, by which we put these people in office. However we cast our ballot, it is our greatest privilege.